The Logic of Christianity

A Syllogistic Chain

Stan A. Lindsay

Published by

Say Press
P.O. Box 691063
Orlando, FL 32869-1063

Stan A. Lindsay

P.O. Box 18756

Panama City Beach, FL 32417

ISBN: 978-0-9914793-4-4

To My Grandchild(ren)

Beginning with Hunter

(So that [t]he[y] will be able to defend the faith)

Contents

Preface

A generation or two ago, in America, it was commonplace for individuals to argue that a given proposition was true simply because the Bible stated it was true. In this generation, such an argument is no longer generally acceptable—a chief exception being in evangelical (Bible-believing) contexts. In evangelical churches and cultures, such arguments are still given credence. Evangelical preachers and teachers engage in sermonizing and argumentation on the assumption that the audience accepts the premise that the Bible is truth, the inspired Word of God. In *ArguMentor* (pp. 101 ff.), I argue that there is logic (or, for Aristotle, LOGOS) even in what we term ETHOS (accepting the truth of a statement simply because one trusts the individual making the statement). Yet, reliance upon the authority of someone's statement (in this case, the author of the Biblical text quoted—with the implicit belief that the author was inspired by God) would be closer to an argument from ETHOS than an argument from LOGOS. And, LOGOS, or logic, is what we are seeking to advance in this book. My discussion of how ETHOS is logical follows:

Even though Aristotle does not include **what he calls *ethos*** in the area of argumentation, he does include **what I refer to as *ethos***, but in other words. In Book I, Chapter 15, of *Rhetoric*, Aristotle discusses types of proofs that are not characterized as "artistic" [or that which is generated by the art of the persuader]. Artistic proofs, for Aristotle, are *ethos*, *pathos*, and *logos*. **Nonartistic proofs** may be *laws*, <u>*witnesses*</u>, and *contracts*. A **witness** must be believable in order to be an effective proof. Therefore, a witness must have what I refer to as *ethos* (expertise and active goodwill). A couple of **adjustments to this description of *ethos***, however, are in order when "witnesses" are considered. First, in place of the term "active goodwill," the term **"disinterested"** applies. Disinterested does not mean "not interested." It means "impartial." Eye witnesses to a crime who are partial to either the victim or the accused may very well be *biased* in their testimony. If a witness is biased, that witness loses some *ethos*. Second, in place of the term "expertise," the **unimpeded opportunity** to have actually witnessed the occurrence without obstruction or impairment, combined with the witness's **strength of perception** (visual acuity, hearing, smelling, touch, taste—as applicable), becomes paramount. One could say that if a given witness to an occurrence had unimpeded opportunity plus strength of perception, that witness becomes an **expert** on what actually occurred. Additionally, if a witness is disinterested, s/he demonstrates a fair amount of **goodwill** to both sides of an issue (*ArguMentor* pp. 110-111).

Can the Bible be logically credited with the *ethos* attributable to a trusted witness in the 21st Century? It already holds that status for evangelical Christians, but these evangelical Christians are addressing an increasingly shrinking evangelical audience. A paradigm shift that took hold at the end of the 19th Century in academia effectively "shifted" the perception of the Bible from "the inspired word of God" to "the verbal creations of various humans." Logically, based upon this shift in perception and the resultant presumption of "human error" (with which, in all candor, I do not agree), I will be following a logical progression, as I write successive chapters—so that readers of this book will be prepared to meet the skeptical audience on its own turf. Aristotle called this logical progression approach a "syllogistic chain" or a "chain of syllogisms." The 20th Century rhetorical giant, Kenneth Burke, called such a syllogistic chain: "syllogistic progressive form." What both geniuses are suggesting with these terminologies is that one must build arguments one upon another. This approach has certainly been used by philosophers, throughout the centuries and millennia. Such an approach was used by the father of Modernism, Rene DesCartes.

Stan A. Lindsay

October 31, 2018

Chapter 1

The Shroud, the Pope, and the Faith Continuum

On May 19, 2015, I came within 15 to 20 feet of what could be minute traces of the actual physical

DNA of Jesus of Nazareth, from the minutes and hours immediately following his death. My wife,

Linda, and I drove a rental car for five hours from Florence, Italy, to Turin, Italy, because the

Cathedral of St. John the Baptist (where the Shroud of Turin is housed) had announced an

Exposition of the Shroud, which would last from April 19, 2015 to June 24, 2015. As it turned

out, we were going to be in Italy during that time. I was presenting a paper at a scholarly

conference in Rome, so I ordered tickets (which were free of charge) to view the Shroud on May

19th. The Cathedral had conducted similar public exhibitions of the Shroud in 1998, 2000, and

2010, but we had no opportunity to view the Shroud in those years. Before we spent a few minutes

in the actual presence of the Shroud, we were shown the evidence contained in the Shroud: Using

a variety of scientific methods, we were able to observe visible signs of a face with thorn wounds around the head, of hands and feet that had been pierced by nails, of a back that had been scourged by whips, of a stab wound in the side--a victim of crucifixion identical to the biblical description of Jesus' crucifixion. But was the crucifixion victim whose shroud was on display actually Jesus of Nazareth? Frankly, I do not know. The Shroud of Turin has been, perhaps, the most studied ancient artifact in history. And, there are plenty of skeptics concerning the authenticity of the Shroud. The presenters of the Exposition acknowledged the contrary arguments. For example, in 1988, carbon dating tests were performed on the cloth. These tests indicated a date of 1290-1350 A.D., but carbon dating testing is not always reliable. Once, carbon dating missed the date of the 4000-year-old wrappings of a mummy by a thousand years. On the other hand, the carbon dating tests could be accurate. One's faith in Christianity need not rest on a belief that the Shroud of Turin is the genuine burial shroud of Jesus. It may be an extremely remote possibility that the Shroud is genuine. Even so, the remotest possibility that Linda and I may have been within 15 to 20 feet of the actual physical DNA of Jesus produced a genuinely moving experience. There were no vocal skeptics at the viewing. Even if this shroud belonged to a crucifixion victim from the 13th or 14th century A.D. (the likelihood of which I am skeptical, since Christianity had, by then, long been the dominant world religion, and it seems highly questionable that someone would have been crucified, at that time, in exactly the same manner as Jesus), still the reality of physical proof of crucifixion wounds of "someone" produced reverence in the entire crowd. The point of the Shroud experience is that one need not have overwhelming faith that the Shroud belonged to Jesus to be moved by it.   Even the tiniest, remotest inkling of a miniscule shred of possibility that we were truly in the physical presence of the DNA of Jesus was awe-inspiring. Even miniscule faith in a tiny possibility is still faith.

Two days prior to viewing the Shroud of Turin, Linda and I were in St. Peter's Square in Vatican City. We had not known before our trip to Rome that Pope Francis would be conducting a canonization that day. The Square was packed with thousands upon thousands of people as the Pope delivered a homily and conducted services in a truly impressive "megachurch." We were half-way back in the crowd of standing-room only spectators in the square. After a couple of hours, it seemed the service was ending. We could see on the big screens posted around the square that the Pope was visiting with a few dignitaries before leaving the scene. Then we heard some cheering in parts of the square. We saw hundreds of hands raising cameras and smart phones in various parts of the square. What was happening? The Pope, after addressing the crowd had decided to ride out through the crowds on some sort of modified golf cart. As the cheers and raised cameras seemed to get closer to us, we took a real interest in the direction in which the cameras were pointed. Then, we saw him. The Pope was riding past us, within about the same 15 to 20 foot proximity that we would later be near the Shroud. I took pictures. Linda took videos. He would stop occasionally to bless someone or kiss a child. I am almost 100% certain that I was within 15 to 20 feet of Pope Francis. As with the Shroud, one's faith in Christianity need not rest on a belief that the Pope is a genuine representative of God. I find myself, often, in disagreement with Pope Francis. There are millions of Christian Protestants who disagree with him. You might even be skeptical about my claim that I was within 15 to 20 feet of the Pope. Even if you saw the pictures I took, you might engage in skepticism, suggesting that I may have Photoshopped the pictures. Even I cannot be 100% certain that I saw him. Perhaps, he has a double. My point is, however, that I have an enormous amount of faith that I was within 15 to 20 feet of the Pope. Although I was pleased (with reservations) to be almost certainly in his presence (as a world-renown representative of Christianity), I was much more moved by that tiny, remote sliver of a possibility that I was in the presence of the physical DNA of Jesus.

Faith is a continuum. It runs all the way from the tiniest, faintest possibility that something is true (such as the faint possibility that I was within 15 to 20 feet of the actual DNA of Jesus) to the almost certain probability that something is true (such as the almost certain fact that I was within 15 to 20 feet of Pope Francis). If I were convinced that there was zero, zilch, zip, nada possibility that the Shroud was genuine, I would probably not have driven to Turin to see it. I would have had absolutely NO faith in it. If I were fully 100% certain that I was within 15 to 20 feet of Pope Francis, I would cease to have "faith" in that proposition. What we "know for certain" is no longer faith. "Faith," as Aristotle explains it, must admit at least two possibilities. In his book, *On Rhetoric*, Aristotle teaches how rhetorical logic works. In rhetoric (as opposed to dialectic), the aim is not to provide absolute truth, but only possible or probable truth. It applies only to matters of which we cannot be 100% certain. Nevertheless, although certainty is impossible, we can logically conclude that something is "probably" or "possibly" true. Aristotle says that the goal of this type of logic is to achieve "faith." If there is no possibility, there is no faith. If there is only one possibility, we call it truth. There is still no faith, because it is absolute truth. John 20:29 records the incident of the Apostle Thomas who demanded, after being told that Jesus was resurrected, that he be allowed to place his fingers in the nail holes in Jesus' hands and his hand in the sword wound in Jesus' side before he would believe. Jesus, after offering the physical terms of proof demanded by Thomas comments: "Because you have seen me, Thomas, you have believed; blessed are those who have not seen, and yet have believed." The logic of Christianity is a faith-based logic. Interestingly, the Bible says: "Without faith it is impossible to please God" (Hebrews 11:6). To understand this type of logic, we must begin by accepting the fact that we could be wrong about various propositions. In cases, for example, of Deliberative Rhetoric (for Aristotle, this means arguments about what can or should happen in the future), Aristotle understands that we cannot really "know" the future, but we can predict things that "possibly" or "probably" will happen. This is Rhetoric. The aim is to produce "faith" that a certain course of action is wiser than another. In cases of Judicial Rhetoric (for Aristotle, this means arguments about what did actually happen in the past—for example, did O. J. actually kill Ron and Nicole?), Aristotle understands that we cannot really "know" for certain what happened, but we can argue persuasively that certain things "possibly" or "probably" did happen. Similarly, when it comes to the logic of Christianity, we are operating in the realm of "faith"—the realm of Rhetoric. We admittedly do not KNOW how the universe came into existence, what happens to us after we die, whether there is meaning in our life, etc., but we can argue logically that our views on these issues are "possible" or "probable."

This chapter is the beginning of a book on the logic of Christianity. I have begun with an illustration of the range of the faith continuum—from the just barely possible to the "almost-certain-but-still-questionable." Notice that even "just barely possible" faith can motivate us to act, as when a terminal cancer patient opts to try a highly suspect experimental treatment, with the hope of beating his/her cancer. On the other hand, even the almost certain (but still slightly questionable) assertion that smoking causes lung cancer can still fail to motivate a given individual to stop smoking. Just the fact that someone has faith in an assertion (such as that smoking causes cancer) does not mean that any given person's actions follow his/her faith. And just the fact that someone's faith in an assertion (such as the experimental cancer treatment) is infinitesimally small does not mean that the person's actions will not follow his/her faith. In the realm of rhetoric, we are all agnostics. The word "agnostic" means we do not know for certain. And, rhetoric (and its logic) are only applied to those issues the truth of which we do not know for certain. In my book *ArguMentor* (p. 7), I discuss a study that demonstrated that even self-avowed atheists were stressed at the prospect of daring God to do harm to their children. Could you, without stress, say the following words: "I dare you, God, to strike my children with terminal cancer"? If you could not do so, without stress, there is at least a tiny, even if infinitesimally small, germ of faith in God inside of you. In Luke 17:6 and Matthew 17:20, Jesus compares faith to a grain of mustard seed. This is a very small grain indeed, but it has great growth potential. Perhaps, as you read this book on the logic of Christianity, your mustard seed will grow.

Chapter 2

Building a Logical Pathway—The Syllogistic Chain

I was born during the first half of the Twentieth Century . . . just barely. Actually, my mother brought me into this world just 22 days before the beginning of the second half of the century--on December 9, 1949. I grew up on a farm not far from New Salem, in Illinois, the pioneer (log cabin) settlement where Abraham Lincoln as a young adult had left his career as a rail splitter, and had begun to study law, a century earlier. In fact, the Sangamon River, which borders New Salem, also bordered my family's farm. The river winds further south from New Salem toward Springfield, the Illinois state capitol, where Lincoln's tomb is located. If we had navigated the Sangamon River by boat from our farm to New Salem (just barely south of Petersburg), we would have been only about 10 miles away, and another 15 or 20 miles from Springfield. Even though I grew up on the banks of the Sangamon, however, I cannot recall anyone ever boating on the river. I recall it being a very muddy river. At least, the land that my dad farmed bordering the river was muddy, but that was a good thing. Our farm was located in what was called the "Sangamon River Bottoms." Johnny Carson used to make jokes about finding a good piece of bottom land, but my dad had actually found it. The rich black soil (mud or silt) in the Sangamon River Bottoms produced excellent crops and a very respectable farm income. In a higher elevation near our house were the bluffs, the original banks of the Sangamon River. The river, over the centuries, had deposited layers and layers of thick black silt (mud) in the river bottoms. That silt contained extremely productive nutrients for crops.

My mom had the job of spending the money the farm brought in. She travelled frequently to downtown Springfield to shop for clothing for the family in some very nice clothing stores. There were occasions when my mom could make this trip to Springfield in a very short period of time, but that was not usually the case. Usually, my mother would need to travel north out of the bottoms to Easton, where she could choose to travel either east or west to catch another highway southward to Springfield. This doubled the travel distance and time. The problem she encountered was that the river that connected our farm to New Salem also provided an obstacle to our travels southward. There was an old Oakford Bridge across the river from the Bottoms, but it had become dilapidated and rusted out and was closed when I was very young. Another bridge from the Bottoms across the Salt Creek toward Greenview was an option, even as I grew to be a young man. This route shaved off one-half hour from the trip to Springfield. The bridge was a rusty iron structure with side retaining walls. Wooden planks were laid across the iron frame and rattled unnervingly as we drove slowly across the single-lane bridge. But even getting to this bridge was a major feat. The only roads that connected our house to this bridge were field roads, which we called "mud roads."

The "primary" roads in the Bottoms were covered with gravel, and other than being very dusty to drive on, were usually passable. But the mud roads were impassable after a rain. The gooey mire would engulf the wheels of the car, if one were to attempt to drive on the road. Even if someone drove a tractor on the wet roads, and was thus able to pass, the tractor tires would leave deep tracks in the mud. Anyone who subsequently attempted to navigate the road (after the mud dried) would be obstructed by the rutted path.

What, you may ask, do mud roads and bad bridges have to do with the logic of Christianity? The story I have related is a representative anecdote. The mud roads and rattling bridge are metaphors for the dilapidated and impassable state of the syllogistic chain that currently exists for Christian logic. The need for logical infrastructure repair and refurbishment for Christianity reaches back to long before my childhood in the middle of the Twentieth Century. The issues come from before Abraham Lincoln's mid-Nineteenth Century reiteration of our founding fathers' (late Eighteenth Century) position that all men are "created" equal. They even predate Martin Luther's Sixteenth Century reformation cry: "Sola Scriptura" (translated: "by scripture alone"). Some pertain to a time earlier than that of Jesus, his disciples, and the New Testament. They go back to the time of Aristotle in the Fourth Century BC, and even earlier—although Aristotle provides a roadmap to get us to where we need to be. The logical refurbishment of Christianity must go back beyond Daniel, Isaiah, King David, and even Moses. This current book is an attempt to resurface some of the mud roads that have become impassable, to repair some crumbling bridges, and to pave the highways that will allow others to more easily follow our logical pathways.   Aristotle calls the various steps one must take to build a logic a "syllogistic chain." In my book, *ArguMentor*, page 165, I describe such a chain:

> [Each link in the] chain of argumentation must be completed before the next one begins. And, so on. And so on. As an arguer, one must build his/her argumentation on facts, statistics, case studies, anecdotes, examples, and syllogisms that others have established. If one moves the argument along by only one link of a chain, it is a successful argument. If one, by supplying a rebuttal for which there is no valid backing, refutes an argument, the refutation is a successful argument, until someone else comes along with a backing or inductive argument or deductive argument that moves the syllogistic chain along.

On page 93, I point out:

> What Aristotle called a chain of syllogisms, Kenneth Burke (1968) called syllogistic progressive form. Syllogistic progressive form simply suggests logic in the development of any literary work. The major premise and at least one minor premise must be established as credible with the audience before conclusions can be drawn. Then, in turn, these newly established conclusions may be employed as premises for other conclusions, until one reaches the final conclusion, the point that the author is ultimately attempting to persuade his/her audience to accept. "In so far as the audience, from its acquaintance with the premises, feels the rightness of the conclusion, the work is formal [meaning that it has syllogistic progressive form]" (124).

As I grew up on the farm in the 1950s and 1960s, I believed (as many Evangelical Christians do, today) that, when arguing theological issues, I could simply appeal, as did Martin Luther, to the scriptures. If the Bible clearly stated a truth proposition, the issue was resolved. In my naïveté, I assumed that the authority of the Bible had long been established for everyone. I felt that the syllogistic chain could begin with the premise that the Bible was authoritative. The only legitimate questions, then, pertained to issues of interpretation of scripture. In my undergraduate years, at a conservative Christian college, I took three years of Hellenistic Greek language courses and two years of Classical Hebrew language courses, in addition to multiple content courses covering Old and New Testament texts. As a master's student in Rabbinic Hebrew at Indiana University, I continued my study of Classical and Mishnaic Hebrew, and added courses in Aramaic and Syriac, in addition to multiple content courses covering Old Testament and Rabbinic texts. My naïveté dissipated rapidly. My Jewish professors and classmates felt no compunction whatsoever to assist me in defending Christianity. Quite to the contrary, I found myself challenged constantly to defend my premises. It was not even a generally accepted premise in a primarily Jewish department that the Hebrew Bible was authoritative—let alone the Greek New Testament! One of my professors warned me that it was proverbial in academia: to earn a master's degree, one must stop believing in the Bible; to earn a Ph.D., one must stop believing in God. When I wrote my master's thesis, I invited a New Testament scholar from the University to be a part of my thesis committee. He offered even more resistance to my notions of the reliability of the New Testament than did my Jewish professors.

What had happened to the Sola Scriptura premise? I began to realize the full extent to which the syllogistic chain of Christianity had been compromised. Over the years, as I watch other young unsuspecting college students face the onslaught of critical Biblical scholarship in religion classes at various universities, I have empathy. I know what they are going through. They are hopelessly mired in a mud road, in the logic of Christianity. They cannot logically argue for the truth of a biblical proposition until they have re-established the premise that the Bible is reliable. This is no mean task. More than a century of concerted scholarly skepticism has targeted the credibility of the various biblical texts. Furthermore, before they could even begin to argue for the correctness of the Bible, they find themselves face-to-face with a crumbling rickety bridge of theism vs. atheism. How can one argue that the God of Judeo-Christian scriptures is the true God, if it has not been successfully argued that there even is a God? And, before one can argue that there is a God, one must grapple with the issue of whether the universe is randomly constituted, or whether there is purposeful action that produced its existence. We find ourselves precisely where Genesis begins—at the beginning of the universe. (How interesting!) We may use Aristotle's concept of syllogistic chains to begin building a logical pathway from there.

Chapter 3

The Four Logical Explosions of Human History

What is a "logical explosion"? The phrase "paradigm shift" was coined by Thomas Kuhn in his 1962 book, *The Structure of Scientific Revolutions*, to describe the fact that scientists do NOT passively allow their thoughts to GRADUALLY change over time, in a linear fashion. Instead, every now and then, there is an "EXPLOSION" that destroys the old paradigm and replaces it with a new paradigm. The scientific community realizes that the paradigm (or pattern of discovering truth) that it had been using is defective. The pattern no longer works satisfactorily to explain reality—as when the notion that the sun revolved around the earth no longer satisfactorily explained the relationship between our planet and sun. In the scientific community, then, a paradigm shift or scientific revolution occurs. The old pattern of detecting reality is discarded and an entirely new pattern takes its place. This is a logical explosion, of sorts. The most recent major paradigm shift that rocked the world occurred somewhere close to the time I was born. It was the shift from Modernism to Postmodernism. (I will consider this Postmodern shift, later, as the Fourth Logical Explosion.) The fact that these paradigm shifts occur is excellent evidence that "action" exists (as opposed to sheer "motion"). The scientists are "agents" who of their own "free will" "act" in accordance with their own "purposes." In order to have "action," according to Kenneth Burke, there must be an "agent" who "acts." That agent must have "free will" to act in accordance with his own "purpose." If there is no free will necessary (as when a bird builds a nest, according to "instinct"--not free will--in the same way every other bird of its species builds it), this is not "action"—it is "motion." A rock tumbling down the hillside is not "acting," but it is "moving." The rock has no free will; it is moving in accordance with the law of gravity. (Nevertheless, if an "agent" with free will "intentionally" kicks the rock to initiate its downward motion, "action" is involved. The agent who kicked the rock "acted.")

Following the terminology of Kuhn's "paradigm shift," but applying it to the broader sphere of the "human" community—not just the "scientific" community, as Kuhn limits his term—I detect four "MAJOR LOGICAL EXPLOSIONS" in human history. These are times when virtually all of humanity discards the old ways of viewing the world and substitutes brand new ways of viewing reality. I call these times "explosions" rather than "shifts" or even "revolutions" because their effects are (seismologically) far greater than even Kuhn's paradigm shifts. They each entail drastic observable behavior changes that appear to affect virtually the entire human population (not just science). The four explosions occurred at 1) the dawn of man, 2) the time of Jesus, 3) the Renaissance, and 4) the middle of the Twentieth Century. Kuhn's paradigm shifts cannot comprise these explosions because science (in Kuhn's sense of the word) did not exist at the dawn of man or at the time of Jesus. Kuhn is useful in pointing to the various tremors (or paradigm shifts) that occurred during the Renaissance and afterward, but the Renaissance itself was the "explosion." Constant "shifts" in the tectonic plates produce minor tremors that constantly reshape the earth, but a gigantic shift or earthquake, such as many fear could happen due to the San Andreas fault, might actually reshape a continent. Just as the asteroid explosion that scientists want to credit with the disappearance of the dinosaur reshaped the physical landscape, so these four logical explosions have reshaped the landscape of human logic.

THE DAWN OF MAN

Before the dawn of man, no carbon-based life forms exercised "action." Only "motion." There was no free will. Botanical and zoological life forms, so far as we can tell, "behaved" only in predictable, instinctive, deterministic ways. I use the term "behave" advisedly. "Behaviorism" relates to "motion;" it is a study of what animals do, not what humans do. According to Kenneth Burke, humans "act," rather than "behave." On page 134 of my book *Implicit Rhetoric: Kenneth Burke's Extension of Aristotle's Concept of Entelechy*, I point out:

> Burke is concerned with the essential nature of mankind (CS 219). He asserts that "a definition of [hu]man is at least implicit in any writer's comments on cultural matters" (LSA 2), and he thereupon serves notice that he rejects the reductionism of the behaviorist view of humankind (DD 11). It is human language which, for Burke, distinguishes humankind from all other animal life. Burke tells his audience at the Heinz Werner Lectures:

> I had in mind the particular aptitude that the human biologic organism has for the learning of conventional symbol systems (such as tribal languages), our corresponding dependence upon this aptitude, and the important role it plays in the shaping of our experience. (DD 15)

. . . I [earlier] consider the issue of determinism and free will in connection with Burke's preference for the term "motive" rather than "cause" as an explanation of human action. . . . [Burke] actually believes that human symbolicity implies free will. Otherwise, he would not have taken "sides against behaviorist reductionism" (DD 11). Yet, Burke accedes to biological determinism insofar as human animality is concerned. Burke locates the deterministic factor for humankind in the realm of human animality. He locates free will in the realm of human symbolicity.

What kinds of "actions" did humans engage in at the dawn of man? Burke has already mentioned the use of symbols (words, language). Animals do not choose the means by which they communicate; humans do. You or I may choose to speak English, German, Spanish, Greek, Hebrew, Italian, French, etc. For an animal, there is no communicative choice. If one is a dog, one barks; a cat meows; a bird chirps; a cow moos, etc. Furthermore, the other members of the animal's species instinctively understand the meaning of the specific animal's communication. Not so, with humans. I do not understand Chinese, Japanese, etc. In addition to language use, Burke notes that humans design and make tools to separate them from their natural condition. Stone Age humans developed stone knives, axes, spear heads, arrows, etc. And, then, they did something with these tools that they had made that indicated an important logical explosion: They "buried" these tools with their dead! Why? The best explanation anthropologists can put forth is that these early humans "believed" in an afterlife and wanted their dead relatives to have access to these tools in that afterlife. This is RELIGION! On page 93 of my book *Disneology: Religious Rhetoric at Walt Disney World*, I observe:

> Anthropologists are interested in human views of the afterlife. Dennis O'Neil, on the website "Evolution of Modern Humans: Archaic Human Culture" (http://anthro.palomar.edu/homo2/mod_homo_3.htm), writes: "The Neandertal ritual burial of their own dead implies a belief in an afterlife. This is basically a rudimentary religious concept. Likewise, the ritual burial of cave bear trophy heads is consistent with a supernatural belief system."

Religious belief (the belief in the afterlife) was the first logical explosion. There were no signs of religious belief anywhere else in the animal world. The term "LOGOS" from which the word logic is formed means "word." A syllogistic chain (or logical sequence) began just as soon as this carbon-based being was able to use "words." The ability to use logic in making words was extended to using logic to make stone tools. And the ability to use logic for making words and tools gave birth to the first "logical" view of human existence in the world: there probably is an afterlife.

Other logical sequences (syllogistic chains) seem to have developed in human cultures:

1. If there is an afterlife, some beings must be living in some realm beyond the mortal human realm.

2. If there are beings who are beyond mortality, they must be superior to mortal humans.

3. If beings that are superior to mortal humans exist, these beings must in some sense be more powerful than humans, and it may be in the best interest of humans to make these beings well-disposed to the weaker mortals.

4. To curry the favor of these more powerful beings, humans should sacrifice animals (and other mortal humans?) to these immortal beings.

Animal (and, sometimes, human) sacrifice developed in virtually every religion on earth. Even the Babylonians, Persians, Greeks, and Romans whose world empires took turns encompassing and ruling over the small religious culture of Israel practiced animal sacrifice, as did Israel . . . UNTIL the time of Jesus.

THE TIME OF JESUS

The death of Jesus, somewhere around 30 A.D., began a logical explosion. For Christians, the logical need for animal sacrifice was annihilated. No longer was any animal sacrifice necessary, because Jesus, as the sacrificial lamb, perfected and thus finished all need for blood sacrifice. The logical explosion ensued, throughout the empire. In 70 A.D., the Jewish temple in Jerusalem was destroyed by Roman legions. The great Jewish religion, which for thousands of years had followed a code of animal sacrifice to atone for sins, immediately and totally ceased all animal sacrifice. Never again would animals be sacrificed in a priestly Jewish religion. Fewer than 300 years later, Constantine decriminalized Christianity and, in 380 A.D., Christianity became the official religion of the Roman Empire. Sacrifices to the Roman pantheon of gods ceased. For a thousand years, the logic of Christianity progressively engulfed the world.

The Christian religion grew like wildfire. The civilized world embraced not only Jesus, but also the entire logical system: his God, the God of Abraham, and the moral code of ancient Judaism, the Ten Commandments (even if all humans in the world—or in the church—did not always obey the code). Even the upstart new religion of Muhammed, in the 7th Century, agreed that the one true God was the God of Abraham. Progressively, all vestiges of early pagan religions were being erased . . . UNTIL the Renaissance.

THE RENAISSANCE

The explosion began when Christians' faith in the promised return of Jesus did not materialize at the time they expected it. John Thomas Didymus, who apparently believes that Christians should accept the conclusion that their hope in the return of Christ might well be mistaken, states the situation fairly in his article "Failed End-of-World Predictions of Jesus' Coming: Montanists and the Ecumenical Council (1000 A.D.)":

> The Ecumenical Council sitting in 999 declared solemnly that the world would end on January 1, 1000 A.D. That was the signal for mass madness. On the last day of the year, St. Peter's at Rome was filled with a crazed mass of people, weeping, trembling, screaming in fear of the Day of the Lord. They thought that God would send fire from heaven and burn the world to ashes. Many rich and wealthy people gave away their possessions to the poor to make heaven. They dressed up in sackcloth and poured ashes over themselves. The grounds of St. Peter's on new

year's eve was filled with people vying to outdo each other in acts of penance and self-mortification, self-mutilation and flagellation. Some branded their skins with hot iron to prove their repentance; some were actually beaten to death by overzealous mates. But new year came and passes [sic] and nothing happened. (Article Source: http://EzineArticles.com/5476263)

And yet, something DID happen—an explosive fuse was lit! Just as it took nearly 400 years to enact the full effects of the logical explosion occurring at Jesus' death, it took roughly 400 years from the disappointment of Jesus' non-return in 1000 to enact the full effects of that logical explosion. The Christianized world had begun (in 1000 A.D.) to lose faith in Christianity as the single source of truth. The Renaissance (dating from the late 14th century A.D.) was a rebirth of interest in classical Greek and Roman culture and philosophy. Humans, world-wide, looked to other humans as the source of truth, as they systematically doubted the truth that was being fed to them by the Church. An extremely important development in this logical explosion of doubt was the work of the philosopher Rene DesCartes. In my book, *Disneology: Religious Rhetoric at Walt Disney World*, page 6, I write:

"The seventeenth century philosopher **Rene DesCartes** . . . is credited with founding **Modernism**. His **methodological doubt** suggested that Realists should doubt everything that could be doubted. Whatever is left is truth. This is the basis of the **scientific method**. Scientists make propositions that they are not entirely certain of. These uncertain propositions are called '**hypotheses**." Scientists, then, attempt to systematically 'doubt' their hypotheses. They conduct experiments, to see if they can disprove the hypotheses. If they cannot doubt the hypotheses, these hypotheses are considered 'truth.' **Empiricists**, following DesCartes, suggested that one could doubt everything that is not *empirically verifiable* (capable of being verified by sense-data—seeing, hearing, smelling, tasting, and feeling)."

In terms of the logic of Christianity, this move was a major blow to Christian faith. Since one cannot see, hear, taste, smell, or touch God, Empiricists—those who rely for evidence of "truth" on the "sense" data of the five empirical senses—could conclude that faith in God is "non-sense" (meaning literally that it is not based on "sense" data).

POSTMODERNISM

Then, I was born (around 1950) and the logical world exploded again (coincidence, not causality!) As it turns out, skepticism can be aimed not only at God and Christianity. It can also be aimed at Empiricism, Science, and even Mathematics. In terms of Empiricism, I can be fooled by my sense of sight, as when I see a mirage in the middle of the road. Hearing can be wrong, as when one has tinnitus—the hearing of sound when no external sound is present. The sense of smell can easily mistake the smell of sulfur water for rotten eggs. The sense of taste can cause one to think s/he has consumed butter, when it is, actually, Parkay margarine. The sense of touch can confuse having walked through hanging threads in a dark haunted house, so that one feels one has encountered spider webs and continues to have them on oneself. I continue, in *Disneology: Religious Rhetoric at Walt Disney World*, pages 6-7:

[E]ven empirical evidence (sense-data) can be doubted, so Empiricism as a Modernist philosophy was largely discredited by the relentless application of methodological doubt. Mathematics was the last stronghold of Modernism. When Kurt Gödel [a friend of Einstein] demonstrated that even mathematics could be doubted—because the whole system proves itself by itself—Modernism effectively crumbled . . . In place of Modernism, Postmodernism arose. Postmodernism could be called a Realistic philosophy in that it makes a truth claim: typically, "there is *no* truth" or "there is *relative* truth." Burke is a Postmodern Realist, but he is not happy with either of these truth-related formulas. In his essay, "The Rhetorical Situation," Burke is much happier with a Postmodern truth-related formula such as "there is *probable* truth." Aristotle teaches that "probable truth" is discovered through *rhetoric*. Christian Realism is close to Burke's Postmodern view that "there is probable truth."

WHAT A LOGICAL EXPLOSION POSTMODERNISM IS! Beginning with the Dawn of Man, humans concluded that an afterlife was logical—there is a realm beyond the grave. With the advent of Christianity, the world shifted from believing in the efficacy of animal sacrifice to please the gods. The truth was to be found in the teachings of the God of Abraham. With the Renaissance, the logical explosion began to abandon God as the source of truth and rediscover truth from human sources. Skepticism became the operative method of discovering truth. Then, around 1950, it became evident that skepticism had become bankrupt. With Gödel's last nail in the coffin of Modernism, Postmodernists concluded that "THERE IS NO TRUTH!!!" What a scene: it is just as if the ultimate Nuclear War had taken place IN LOGIC! Instead of the pictures of the smoldering Los Angeles ruins from the *Terminator* movies, visualize the barren smoldering ruins of anything resembling logical truth. But, Burke points out that one cannot LOGICALLY say "There is no truth" because that statement is, itself, a TRUTH CLAIM! If there is no truth, the statement that "there is no truth" CANNOT BE TRUE! Those (illogical) Postmodernists who persist in clinging to the (illogical) statement that "there is no truth" continue to attempt to disparage the logic of Christianity, saying that it cannot be true, because there is NO truth. The only logical way out of this malaise is Burke's formula: THERE IS PROBABLE TRUTH. If there is PROBABLE truth, we can reintroduce empirical data into the argument. But, we can also reintroduce non-empirical data—the logic that seems to be implicit in humanity since the dawn of man: that God and the afterlife do exist. We return full circle.

But, the new ground rules for logical argument are in the field of Rhetoric, not the field of Philosophy. I repeat what I stated in Chapter 1:

> In his book, *On Rhetoric*, Aristotle teaches how rhetorical logic works. In rhetoric (as opposed to dialectic), the aim is not to provide absolute truth, but only possible or probable truth. It applies only to matters of which we cannot be certain. Nevertheless, although certainty is impossible, we can logically conclude that something is "probably" or "possibly" true. Aristotle says that the goal of this type of logic is to achieve "faith." . . . [And, as] the Bible says: "Without faith it is impossible to please God" (Hebrews 11:6).

The next link in this logical syllogistic chain, then is to argue that "action" took place before there was "human" action. We will turn to the "intelligent design" debate to establish that some agent was using "action" in the formation of the universe.

Chapter 4

Lights! Camera! Action!

Very well, I will stipulate that the CAMERA was invented by humans (although, the principle by which the camera works has been known since before the time of Aristotle, who, in the 4th Century BC, observed the crescent of a solar eclipse by allowing the light to proceed through a hole of a sieve), but I DO CONTEND that LIGHT AND ACTION definitely preceded the Dawn of Man. Even advocates of the Big Bang Theory will stipulate that LIGHT itself goes back to the very beginning of the universe. The issue related to ACTION is a little trickier.

As I mentioned in Chapter 3, in order to have "action," according to Kenneth Burke, there must be an "agent" who "acts." That agent must have "free will" to act in accordance with his own "purpose." A basic premise of the Big Bang Theory and the Theory of Evolution is that the universe and all life forms were spontaneously generated WITHOUT the help of any Agent/higher being. How could anyone ever possibly prove such a premise? One could certainly never prove such a premise using the scientific skepticism of Modernism. How could an experiment be devised to test the hypothesis? There is no way to reproduce the circumstances and test them by experiment. The most that scientific Modernism could accomplish was to be skeptical of the premise that the universe and all life forms WERE generated by the "agency" of some higher being. But, being skeptical does not produce knowledge. As we have learned in the paradigm shift from Modernism to Postmodernism, skepticism has simply demolished the hope that humans can ever discover absolute knowledge or truth. Until it is possible for someone to TIME TRAVEL back to the beginning of the universe or the beginning of life forms, whether an intelligent being "acted" in the formation of the universe or in the generation of life forms must remain among those issues with which Rhetoric deals: matters about which we debate. Aristotle, in *Rhetoric* I.2.xii, asserts: "[W]e debate about things that seem to be capable of admitting two possibilities" (Kennedy [1991] translation). So, welcome to the debate over whether ACTION was involved in the generation of the universe and life! As Aristotle requires, the issue of whether ACTION was present early in the universe admits two possibilities: **POSSIBILITY 1.** That the universe came into existence without any Action, or **POSSIBILITY 2.** That the universe came into existence by the Action of an Agent.

What sorts of PROOFS may we use to assert that the universe came into existence by the Action of an Agent?

PROOF 1. Syllogistic, deductive logic (which we will consider later),

PROOF 2. Empirical evidence (which we will consider later), and

PROOF 3. Something that one of the key rhetoricians of the Twentieth Century, Richard

Weaver, called "THE METAPHYSICAL DREAM."

We begin with this third proof; then, we will move to the second proof and finally to the first proof.

PROOF 3. THE METAPHYSICAL DREAM

Richard Weaver has earned a great deal of respect in the field of Rhetoric. As a Professor at the

University of Chicago, Weaver and Burke had some contact. They were by no means friends, but

they both agreed that humans (as distinct from other animals) are symbol-using, and that they are

beings of choice and free will. Sonja K. Foss, Karen A. Foss, and Robert Trapp, in their widely-

acclaimed book *Contemporary Perspectives on Rhetoric* (30th Anniversary Edition) review and

analyze ten "thinkers who have exerted a profound influence on contemporary rhetorical theory."

Among these 20th Century thinkers are Kenneth Burke, Chaim Perelman, Stephen Toulmin,

Michel Foucault, and Richard Weaver. Weaver, in his book *Ideas Have Consequences*, posits that

a level of knowledge exists for human beings that is "an intuitive feeling about the immanent

nature of reality" (page 18). He calls this level of knowledge "the metaphysical dream." Burke,

while he resists having his own personal critical method "characterized as 'intuitive' and

'idiosyncratic,' epithets that make (him) squirm" (PLF 68), DOES (at the same time) CREDIT

animals with possessing "an INTUITIVE signaling system" as their form of communication

("Motion, Action, and the Human Condition," p. 79). It seems LOGICAL (using argument from

analogy) that, if even ANIMALS have INTUITION, certain concepts that humans hold to be true might also come to humans primarily through "an INTUITIVE feeling about the immanent nature of reality." For example, one cannot empirically prove that such a thing as "JUSTICE" exists. The concept is an INTUITIVE feeling. We "INTUITIVELY feel" that JUSTICE exists when one who has committed a "wrong" receives some sort of punishment. But where do we get the idea that "WRONG" exists? We "INTUITIVELY feel" that someone who takes advantage of another because of his or her superior intellect, physical strength, or skill is somehow doing something "WRONG." Why else do we protect children from adult advertisers who might exert persuasive methodologies? Why do we have laws against stealing, rape, murder, etc.? "INTUITIVELY," we "feel" that such "acts" are "WRONG." And yet, in the animal world (comparing humans "empirically" to other animals), no such "INTUITIVE feelings" of "right and wrong" or "justice" exist. Animals that are larger or stronger feel no shame about preying on smaller or weaker animals. Alpha males seize females at their own discretion. There is no concept of rape. From where does our concept of "free will" come? Are these concepts not the result of "an intuitive feeling about the immanent nature of reality"?

When humans began to bury their dead, and to bury artifacts along with them, "an intuitive feeling about the immanent nature of reality" was operative. In the fact that 99% of all humans who have ever lived on planet Earth have believed that superior beings/gods exist who have free will to ACT relative to humans on Earth, "an intuitive feeling about the immanent nature of reality" is operative. What is particularly interesting is that, even science-oriented humans such as astronomer Carl Sagan, who refuse to admit the possible existence of a divine being, are somehow convinced that superior beings (aliens) from other planets do exist. This is just further evidence of "an intuitive feeling about the immanent nature of reality" that cannot seem to dismiss the possibility/probability of the existence of beings who are superior to humans.

In the Modern Period (from the 17th century to midway through the 20th century)—the period which Stephen Toulmin decries as the hegemony of theoretical argument—and most especially in the portion of that period dominated by Empiricism, such talk of "an intuitive feeling about the immanent nature of reality" would be dismissed, out of hand. But, we are no longer living under the super-skepticism of Modernism. We live in the period of Postmodernism, in which the bankruptcy of philosophical Empiricism must be acknowledged. But, the belief in someone who ACTED in the formation of the universe is CERTAINLY NOT DEVOID OF EMPIRICAL EVIDENCE.

PROOF 2. EMPIRICAL EVIDENCE

The amount of EMPIRICAL (sense) data that may be used to argue for the existence of ACTION in the formation of the world is growing exponentially, in our generation. But EMPIRICAL data has long been cited as evidence of divine ACTIVITY. The shepherd-poet-lyricist-singer-turned-king, David, the author of many of the Psalms in the Hebrew Bible cites EMPIRICAL evidence in his poetic proclamations that God was easily detected in the formation of the universe:

Psalm 8:3 states: "I observe Your heavens, the work of Your fingers, the moon and the stars that You have established."

Psalm 19:1-6 elaborates:

> The heavens declare the glory of God, and the skies show forth his handiwork. Day after day, they speak; night after night, they declare knowledge. There is no language system that does not hear their voice. Their measuring line stretches throughout the whole Earth; their words reach to the ends of the world. In the heavens He has placed a home for the sun, like a bridegroom who goes forth or an athlete running a race, it rises at one end of the heavens, and completes its circuit to the other end.

In Psalm 65:9-13, he notices the regular cycles of rain and agricultural growth:

> You visit the land and water it . . . . You provide grain, for so You have ordained it, watering the furrows, softening the ridges. You make it soft with showers [and] bless its vegetation. The pastures . . . hills . . . and meadows are clothed with flocks and the valleys are covered with grain.

In Psalm 104:10-30, he observes the balance and cyclical renewing of nature:

> He sends forth springs into the valleys; they run among the mountains; they give drink to every beast of the field . . . . By them the birds of the heavens have their habitation . . . . The earth is filled with the fruit of Your works. He causes the grass to grow for the cattle, and herb for the service of man, and oil to make his face to shine, and bread that strengthens man's heart. . . . The cedars of Lebanon . . . where the birds make their nests: As for the stork, the fir-trees are her house. The high mountains are for the wild goats; the rocks are a refuge for the rock-badgers. He appointed the moon for seasons: The sun knows its going down; You make darkness/night . . . wherein all the beasts of the forest creep forth. The young lions roar after their prey and seek their food from God. The sun rises and they get away and lay down in their dens. Then, man goes forth to his work and to his labor until

evening. . . . The earth is full of Your riches. Yonder is the sea, great and wide, wherein are innumerable creeping things, both small and great beasts. . . . These all wait for You that you may give them their food in due season. You give and they gather. . . . You take away their breath and they die. You send forth Your Spirit and they are created. You renew the face of the ground.

In Psalm 139:14-16, he empirically considers human life and is impressed: "I will give You thanks, for I am fearfully and wonderfully made: Wonderful are Your works . . . . My frame was not hidden from you when I was made in secret . . . . Your eyes did see my unformed substance."

I cite the Psalms as textual evidence that ACTION was observed (by a shepherd) in the physical world, thousands of years ago. The EMPIRICAL evidence of logical ACTION is quite strong. The amount of EMPIRICAL (sense) data that may be used to argue for the existence of ACTION in the formation of the world is growing exponentially, these days. Why? Because technology has enabled us to SEE more of the physical universe than was ever possible for David or his predecessors. NASA's New Horizons space craft reports from near Pluto. The Hubble Telescope gives us EMPIRICAL glimpses of galaxies, far, far away. Genetic researchers study the codes of biological forms. Atomic scientists investigate the very structure of atoms. And, every element of new EMPIRICAL data discovered reiterates the same message handed down from David's humble observations: There is ACTION in the universe. Ours is not a world of random motion. From galaxies to atoms, entropy (or the tendency to decline into disorder) is SYSTEMATICALLY arrested. The centrifugal force that would tend to cause the Earth to fly away from the sun (as you tended to be drawn outward from your spinning merry-go-round, as a child) is carefully balanced by the centripetal force (gravity) of the sun. Likewise, the moon is balanced to avoid entropy from the Earth. Likewise, every minute atom in the universe is balanced to avoid entropy, until we humans split the atoms and release untold energy. Genetic research discovers "CODES" or LANGUAGE MESSAGES that tell our bodies whether to be male or female, black, brown, yellow, red or white, short or tall, blond or brunette, inclined or immune to certain ailments, etc. Who wrote the language? Who wrote the code? Can codes just WRITE THEMSELVES? The logic of Christianity argues that the likelihood of some intelligent being ACTING in the universe is tremendous.

PROOF 1. SYLLOGISTIC, DEDUCTIVE LOGIC

So, the rhetorical syllogism looks like this:

<u>MAJOR PREMISE</u>: EVERY INSTRUMENT KNOWN TO MAN THAT IS MADE WITH SYSTEMATIC WORKING PARTS THAT OPERATE IN AN "ORDERLY" FASHION, AND THAT HANDLE THE PROBLEM OF ENTROPY AND TAKE MEASURES TO AVOID ENTROPY ARE THE RESULT OF SOMEONE'S "ACTION."

(Conversely, if there is no "order," the instrument moves randomly, and without purpose, "motion"—but not "action"—is involved. Compare, for example, a clock with a rock.)

<u>MINOR PREMISE</u>: GALAXIES, SOLAR SYSTEMS, THE EARTH AND ITS MOON, VEGETABLE LIFE FORMS, ANIMAL LIFE FORMS, HUMAN LIFE FORMS, ATOMS, ETC. ARE MADE WITH SYSTEMATIC WORKING PARTS THAT OPERATE IN AN "ORDERLY"

FASHION, AND THAT HANDLE THE PROBLEM OF ENTROPY AND TAKE MEASURES TO AVOID ENTROPY.

<u>CONCLUSION</u>: GALAXIES, SOLAR SYSTEMS, THE EARTH AND ITS MOON, VEGETABLE LIFE FORMS, ANIMAL LIFE FORMS, HUMAN LIFE FORMS, ATOMS, ETC. ARE THE RESULT OF SOMEONE'S "ACTION."

This is the logical conclusion of scientists, mathematicians, and philosophers who subscribe to the theory of "Intelligent Design." It is also the logical conclusion of some very well-respected authorities. One mathematician who theorized (based on principles of modal logic) that a higher being must exist was (the close friend of Albert Einstein) Kurt Gödel, who died in 1978 after driving the last nail in the coffin of Modernism. You don't find mathematicians who are more highly respected than Gödel. For his part, Einstein said in 1954: "I do not believe in a personal God and I have never denied this but have expressed it clearly. If something is in me which can be called religious, then it is the unbounded admiration for the structure of the world so far as our science can reveal it." He once remarked to a young physicist: "I want to know how God created this world, I am not interested in this or that phenomenon, in the spectrum of this or that element. I want to know His thoughts; the rest are details." Fair enough. The only link in the logical chain we seek to establish, at this point, is that intelligent ACTION is evident in the structure of the universe. Other famous scientists who have expressed the belief that the structure of the universe argues for a belief in the ACTION of a superior being are Copernicus, Bacon, Galileo, Newton, and even Descartes. But, none of these were specifically advocates of the theory of "Intelligent

Design." Why? Partly because the intelligent design movement began after these scientists had died. The intelligent design movement began in earnest in the early 1990s with Phillip E. Johnson's book, *Darwin on Trial*. Essentially, the movement began in order to create an alliance among scientists who believed in a theistic explanation of the design of the universe. A primary goal of the movement was to defend and promote the teaching of a theistically based view of the beginnings of life and the universe in the Public School systems to counterbalance the teaching of evolutionary theory. The National Academy of Sciences, issued a policy statement saying "Creationism, intelligent design, and other claims of supernatural intervention in the origin of life or of species are not science because they are not testable by the methods of science." That statement is probably true enough; but just as true is the statement "The claims of EVOLUTIONARY THEORY in the origin of life or of species are not science because they are not testable by the methods of science." As I stated at the beginning of this chapter: Until someone can TIME TRAVEL back to the beginning of the universe or the beginning of life forms, whether or not an intelligent being "acted" in the formation of the universe or in the generation of life forms must remain among those issues with which RHETORIC deals: matters about which we debate. NEITHER evolutionary theory nor intelligent design is testable by scientific methods.

The conclusions of many EXPERTS who have seriously grappled with the issue of this debate is that SOMEONE "ACTED" IN THE FORMATION OF GALAXIES, SOLAR SYSTEMS, THE EARTH AND ITS MOON, VEGETABLE LIFE FORMS, ANIMAL LIFE FORMS, HUMAN LIFE FORMS, ATOMS, ETC. Is this the conclusion of EVERYONE? No. But, that is the nature of rhetorical argument. The logic of Christianity is based upon rhetorical argument—dealing with matters that cannot be known for certain, but only probably or possibly. If you grant the possibility or probability that "ACTION" was present in the formation of the world, you have some level of "faith." We next turn to the second link in the syllogistic chain: that there is a God.

Chapter 5

The God of Logic vs. Jeffrey Dahmer

Given the premise that the universe was formed via (logical, purposeful) ACTION, it is a simple deduction that SOMEONE with "logic" and "purpose" ACTED. This was an easy syllogistic deduction for the ancient Greek philosophers, as well. The fact that the Greeks used the same word (LOGOS) to mean both "logic" and "word" is instructive. The ancient Greek School of Philosophy Stoicism (from around 300 BC) named God "LOGOS"—the ACTIVE logic that animates the universe. Christianity agrees. John 1:1-3 states: "In the beginning was LOGOS, and LOGOS was with God, and LOGOS was God. The same was in the beginning with God. All things were made through [LOGOS]; and without [LOGOS] was not anything made that has been made." Before the time of the Stoics, Heraclitus (from around 535-475 BC), notices the link between "rational speech" and the "universe's rational structure." For him, LOGOS was that link. The Jewish philosopher Philo of Alexandria (20 BC-50 AD), a contemporary of both Jesus and the author of the Gospel of John, writes of the LOGOS of God as "the bond of everything, holding all things together and binding all the parts and prevent[ing] them from being dissolved and separated." (Philo's comments sound like an early recognition of the tendency toward entropy, as well as a recognition that LOGOS controls the tendency.) While the Book of Genesis was certainly not dependent upon Greek philosophy, it is striking that the very first chapter of the Bible presents creation in a "logical" order and claims that most steps in the creation and (logical) structuring process were tied to a creative "word." Logic and Word go hand-in-hand in the formation of the universe, the Earth, and its inhabitants. Yet none of those inhabitants of the Earth were capable of exercising anything remotely resembling the LOGOS--the "rational speech" in comprehending and understanding the "universe's rational structure" of which Heraclitus writes--until the advent of man. It is this (unique among carbon-based beings) capacity to exercise LOGOS that makes man "the image of God" (Genesis 1:26).

KENNETH BURKE'S PENTAD: THE JEFFRY DAHMER COUNTER-EXAMPLE

Kenneth Burke teaches a five-pronged cyclical logical schema that advances the simple syllogism. He observes that there are five requirements for the performance of any "act"—whether the act is good, evil, or somewhere in between: Scene, Act, Agent, Agency, and Purpose. He calls these five terms his Pentad and suggests that these terms form a logical "cycle" of terms implicit in an act. Logically, if an Agent performs an Act within a certain Scene, the Agent would use only Agencies available in that Scene to perform the Act, for example. Therefore, the terms tend to be CONSISTENT, and any time there appears to be an INCONSISTENCY, the cycle is regenerated to produce MORE CONSISTENCY. To use an extremely evil example of action, consider Jeffrey

Dahmer—the notorious serial killer, sex offender, and cannibal who raped, murdered, and dismembered seventeen men and boys and engaged in necrophilia and cannibalism with their corpses. Despite the evil nature of his purpose, his actions were entirely CONSISTENT. The world would not have been shocked, then, if a news report of Dahmer in prison told of Dahmer murdering a fellow inmate, sexually abusing his corpse, and even cannibalizing his victim. It would have seemed consistent to the world who knew him. The AGENT (Dahmer) would be "consistent" with such an ACT (murder). And, while the SCENE had changed from Dahmer's apartment (where many of his murders occurred), the prison scene would not seem "inconsistent" with a murder. The AGENCIES by which Dahmer murdered before his incarceration varied— blunt force, punching, strangulation, drugging, knives, etc. Some of these agencies might be available in the prison scene—no inconsistencies—but there also might be additional agencies that are found in the prison scene. The PURPOSE for which Dahmer murdered appears to be sexually related, with additional cannibalistic intent. Cannibalism in prison might have shocked us, but prison is often associated with the types of sexual purpose that Dahmer preferred—male homosexual purposes. In short, Dahmer's ACT would be "logical."

What, then, should one make of the report from May, 1994, that Jeffrey Dahmer had chosen to be baptized in the prison whirlpool by Roy Ratcliff, a minister of the Church of Christ, and a graduate of Oklahoma Christian University? Did the AGENT (Dahmer) change his character? It is possible. Did the AGENT only cynically pretended to convert to Christianity, as a way of becoming more acceptable to society? That is also possible. These possibilities go to an explanation of the PURPOSE of Dahmer in being baptized. Is there anything pertaining to the "death" imagery of immersion baptism (death-burial in water-resurrection from the water) that makes baptism an attractive ACT for Dahmer? Does Dahmer's earlier request for a Bible in his cell (something that was possible in his SCENE) indicate a change in AGENCY? What is happening? We will probably never know. And, it is unnecessary for me to speculate, here, to make my point. Six months later, Dahmer was murdered by a fellow prisoner, on a work detail. Whichever explanation is offered for Dahmer's baptism, the common denominator in all explanations is LOGICAL CONSISTENCY. Whether or not the AGENT converted from serial murderer and cannibal to Christian, all explanations attempt to make logical scenarios. We are gripped by the logic of Burke's Pentad.

THE PENTADIC VIEW OF GOD

In huge contrast to the life-denying ACTS of Jeffrey Dahmer, the ACTS of the AGENT who was involved in the formation of the universe are immensely more life-affirming. While Dahmer destroyed life and consumed and abused corpses, the AGENT whom the Stoics called LOGOS generated life. From the simplest single-celled plant life to the most elaborate animal life, the LOGOS infused every life form with reproductive capacity, so that as one cell or even one life form aged and died, it was replaced with multiple regenerated cells or reproduced entelechies to keep the multiple life forms alive. Furthermore, in symbiotic complexity, as one carbon-based life form died, its cells were consumed and metabolized by other carbon-based life forms, to support life in all of its variations. The purely physical aspects of the universe were coordinated with precision to enable symbiosis to be sustained. The solar warmth combined with the Earth's minerals and with water and oxygen to sustain life. What kinds of ACTS are CONSISTENT with such an AGENT? Logical, rational, life-affirming ACTS. What AGENCIES would be   used by such an AGENT in performing such ACTS? Rational thought and communication, i.e. LOGOS. Whether the AGENT "spoke," as Genesis suggests, or simply communicated the messages implicitly in nature, studies of genetic code, atomic theory, astronomic principles, etc. contend that this agent "communicated" in some fashion. LOGOS is rational communication. For what PURPOSE, then did the LOGOS perform life-affirming ACTS through the AGENCY of Communication?   In other words, what PURPOSE would motivate an AGENT capable of ACTING to create and sustain life forms through the AGENCY of LOGOS to do so?

Abraham Maslow might term such a PURPOSIVE motive as "self-actualization." The AGENT, called LOGOS by the Stoics created logically-reproducing life forms "because it could." And, given the existence of human AGENTS who are capable of ACTION, themselves, we must assume that this self-actualization PURPOSE extended to the desire/PURPOSE of creating and sustaining other AGENTS who (like itself) were also capable of ACTION, COMMUNICATION, and forms of CREATION. From Maslow's motivational theory, we see that motives include not only the ultimate motive of self-actualization, but also the social motive. If the LOGOS could create a being, similar to itself, capable of ACTION and COMMUNICATION, that LOGOS must also have a SOCIAL PURPOSE/motive. The SCENE, then, into which the LOGOS introduced humans was one that, while logical and systematic, lacked SOCIAL INTERACTION. It is altogether CONSISTENT that LOGOS THE AGENT used LOGOS THE AGENCY to self-actualize in the ACT of creating a LOGICAL UNIVERSE capable of sustaining LIFE and, consequently, leading to a SCENE in which SOCIAL PURPOSE motivated the AGENT to create a CREATIVE,

COMMUNICATIVE, ACTION-BASED life form with which LOGOS THE AGENT could communicate.

So, here are the links in the syllogistic chain we have attempted, thus far, to forge:

1. Our syllogistic chain is of the variety found in Rhetoric (the enthymeme) rather than Dialectic. It is faith-based, in the Aristotelian sense. This is not blind faith; rather, it is faith based upon proofs and results in the agreement of all sides to possibility and probability.

2. This type of (rhetorical) proof is all that is truly left to us after the logical explosion that demolished Modernism and brought us Postmodernism.

3. Action exists in the world, as evidenced by the difference between human "action" and animal "motion."

4. Action vastly predated the advent of humans, as the very universe yields evidence of rational logical action.

5. Since an AGENT ACTED using the AGENCY of LOGOS in the formation of the universe, we may logically analyze that action to be motivated by both a self-actualization PURPOSE and a social PURPOSE.

We turn, next, to a consideration of what theologies, present in the universe, would best exemplify this logical description of God.

Chapter 6

WHODUNNIT?

If the God of Logic exists—that is, an "agent" who "acts" in forming and animating the universe in "logical order," using "rational communication," in the process of accomplishing the personal "motives" of achieving "self-actualization" and developing "social" relationships—who is this God? The board game Clue® allows one to win that game, partly, by identifying all potential suspects and, then. systematically eliminating each one until one has come up with the correct "agent" who "killed Mr. Boddy." Like any good murder mystery novel, film, or television show in which the suspects are identified, scrutinized, and gradually, systematically, eliminated from consideration, we may refer to the game of Clue® as a "Whodunnit" (or, as it is more commonly spelled, "Whodunit"). Although I apologize for the fact that the term "Whodunnit" carries with it the connotation of the "agent" being involved in the commission of a crime (and, certainly, "creating and animating the universe" is not considered to be a crime by any serious person), the same procedure that is used in Whodunnits may be logically employed for identifying which "god suspect" most logically should be credited with the formation of the universe.

THE LIST OF SUSPECTS

The game of Clue® offers a finite list of possible suspects: Miss Scarlett, Colonel Mustard, Mrs. White, Mr. Green, Mrs. Peacock, and Professor Plum. Likewise, we may come up with a finite list of possible "god suspects." It seems that, since the God we seek to identify uses "rational communication" for the purpose of developing "social" relationships with the only species to whom that God has given the ability to engage in creative "action"—namely, the human—the God we seek to identify should have, at least at some point, "communicated socially" with this human species. Marketing communication professors Moriarty, Mitchell, and Wells correctly point out that "everything communicates" (p. 55), and, as I pointed out in Chapter 4: "The shepherd-poet-lyricist-singer-turned-king, David, the author of many of the Psalms in the Hebrew Bible, cites EMPIRICAL evidence in his poetic proclamations that God was easily detected in the formation of the universe." This suggests that any objective observer of nature receives some communication from God, but that is not the kind of communication that is required when we suggest that the correct "god suspect" should have, at some point, "communicated socially" with this human species. If this empirical communication were the only form of communication used by the "god suspect," we might be inclined to agree with the assessment of Albert Einstein which I pointed out in Chapter 3: "I do not believe in a personal God and I have never denied this but have expressed it clearly. If something is in me which can be called religious, then it is the unbounded admiration for the structure of the world so far as our science can reveal it . . . I want to know how God created this world, I am not interested in this or that phenomenon, in the spectrum of this or that element. I want to know His thoughts, the rest are details." Naturally, Einstein CAN be wrong on some details. Logically, a God capable of and motivated to communicate socially with a species that that God designed and formed to be capable of similar communicative action would be expected to engage in such social communication. Therefore, an objective thinker might logically conclude that the identity of the correct "god suspect" would be known to mankind, being one of the gods identified by various human cultures throughout history. But who are these gods? The list is still finite, but fairly extensive. [FEEL FREE TO SKIM OVER THE GOD LISTS BELOW TO ARRIVE AT FURTHER COMMENTARY.] If one were to play the GAME OF CLUE with these characters, here is the list of characters you might include in your game:

Our list of "god suspects" includes the following **MESOPOTAMIAN GODS** (from a list supplied by the *Ancient History Encyclopedia* http://www.ancient.eu/article/221/the-mesopotamian-pantheon/): ABGAL (aka, Apkallu), Adapa (the first man) Uan-dugga, En-me-duga, En-me-galanna, En-me-buluga, An-enlilda and Utu-abzu, ABSU (aka, Apsu and Abzu), ADAD, Shala, ADRAMELECH, Anamelech, AJA (aka, Aya), AMURRU (aka, Amurru and Martu), Beletseri, ANSHAR, ANTUM, ANU, (aka, An), Antu, ANUNNAKI, ANZU (aka, Zu and Imdugud), ARAZU, ARURU, ASHNAN, ASHUR, BABA (aka, Bau or Bawa), Lagash, BASMU, BEL, BELIT-TSERI, BIRDU, BULL OF HEAVEN (aka, Gugalanna), BULL-MAN, CARA, DAGON (aka, Dagan), DAMU, DAMKINA, DILMUN, DUMUZI, EA/ENKI, ELLIL, EMESH, ENBILULU, ENKIMDU, ENKIDU, ENLIL, ENMESSARA, ENTEN, Enmesh, ERESHKIGAL (aka, IRKALLA), ERRAGAL, ERIDAN, ERRA/IRRA, ESEMTU, ETANA, Balih, ETEMMU,

GALLA, Igalima, GARRA (aka, Gerra), GESHTINANNA, GESHTU (aka, Geshtu-e), GIBIL, GILGAMESH (depicted as either human or god), GISHIDA (aka, Ningishzida), GUGALANNA, GULA, GUSHKIN-BANDA, HAIA, HUMBABA, IGIGI, IMDUGUD, Pazusu, INANNA (aka, Innina), ISARA, ISHKUR, ISHTAR, ISHUM, KABTA, KI, KISHAR, KITTU, KULITTA, KULLA, KULULLU, KUSAG, KUR, LAHAR, LAHMU and LAHAMU, LAMA (aka, Lamassu), LAMASHTU, LAMASSU, LUGALBANDA, MAGILUM BOAT (aka, The Boat of the West), MAMMETUM (aka, Mamitu), MARDUK, Irra, MISHARU, MUMMU, Ea Mummu, MUSHDAMMA, Ninhursag, MUSHHUSHSHU, MYLITTA, NABU, NAMMU, NAMTAR, NANA, NANAJA, NANNA-SEUN, NANSHE, NEDU, NERGAL, NETI, NIDABA, NIN-AGAL, NINGAL, NINGISHZIDA (aka, Geshida), NINGIZZIA, NINHURSAG (aka, Belet-Ili, Damgalnunna, Nintu, Nintur, Mami and Mama), NIN-ILDU, NINKASI (aka, Ninkar), NINLIL (aka, Sud), Ninazu, NINSHAR, Enshar, NINSHUBUR, NINSUN, NINURTA (aka, Ishkur), NIRAH, NISSABA, NUSKU, PAPSUKKEL, PAZUZU, QUEEN OF THE NIGHT, Liltu, QUINGU (aka, Kingu), RAMMAN (aka, Rimmon, SAKKAN (aka, Sumuqan), SCORPION PEOPLE, SEBITTI, SHAMASH, SHARA, SHERIDA, SHULPAE, SHUTU, SIDURI, SILILI (aka, The Divine Mare), SIN (aka, Nannar), SUMUQAN (aka, Sakkan), SUMUGAN (aka, Shumugan), TABLETS OF DESTINY, TAMMUZ, TIAMAT, TIAMAT'S CREATURES, Musmahhu, Usumgallu, Basmu, Ugallu, Uridimmu, Girtablullu, Umu-Debrutu, Kusarikku, UMMANU, Enuma Elish, Edana, UMUNMUTAMKAG, URSHANABI, USMU (aka, Isimud), UTNAPISHTIM (aka, Ziusudra), UTTU, UTU (aka, Shamash), ZABABA, ZAKAR (aka, Zaqar), ZARPANIT (aka, Beltia), ZALTU, and ZU.

Our list of "god suspects" also includes the following **GREEK GODS** (from a list supplied by the *WikiPagan* http://pagan.wikia.com/wiki/List_of_Deities): Aphrodite, Apollo, Ares, Artemis, Athena, Demeter, Dionysus, Eris, Eos, Gaia, Hades, Hekate, Helios, Hephaestus, Hera, Hermes, Hestia, Pan, Poseidon, Selene, Uranus, and, of course, Zeus. Then, there are the **ROMAN GODS**: Apollo, Ceres, Cupid, Diana, Janus, Juno, Jupiter, Maia, Mars, Mercury, Minerva, Neptune, Pluto, Plutus, Proserpina, Venus, Vesta, and Vulcan. Add to these the **EGYPTIAN GODS**: Anubis, The Aten, Atum, Bast, Bes, Geb, Hapi, Hathor, Heget, Horus, Imhotep, Isis, Khepry, Khnum, Maahes, Ma'at, Menhit, Mont, Naunet, Neith, Nephthys, Nut, Osiris, Ptah, Ra, Sekhmnet, Sobek, Set, Tefnut, and Thoth. Other **AFRICAN GODS** include: Obatala, Yemaya, Chango, Oshun, Elegua, Oya, Ogun, Babalu-Aye', Ochosi, and Osain. **INCAN GODS** include: Inti, Kon, Mama Cocha, Mama Quilla, Manco Capac, Pachacamac, Viracocha, and Zaramama. **AZTEC GODS** include Quetzalcoatl and Tlaloc. **IRISH GODS** include: Angus, Belenos, Brigid, Dana, Lugh, Dagda, Epona, Manannán mac Lir, and Kel. **ANGLO-SAXON GODS** include: Elves, Eostre, Frigg, Hretha, Saxnot, Shef, Thunor, Tir, Weyland, and Woden. **NORSE GODS** include: Asgard, Alfar, Balder, Beyla, Bil, Bragi, Byggvir, Dagr, Disir, Eir, Fenrir, Forseti, Freyja/Freya, Freyr, Frigga, Heimdall, Hel, Hoenir, Idunn, Jord, Lofn, Loki, Mani, Njord, Norns, Verdandi, Urd, Skuld, Nott, Odin, Ran, Saga, Sif, Siofn, Skadi, Snotra, Sol, Syn, Ull, Thor, Tyr, Var, Vali, Vidar, and Vor. **LUSITANIAN GODS** include: Endovelicus, Ataegina, and Runesocesius. **ARMENIAN GODS** include: Anahit, Astghik, and Vahagn. **SLAVIC GODS** include Belobog and Chernobog. Throw in **AFRICAN GODS** (Obatala, Yemaya, Chango, Oshun, Elegua, Oya, Ogun, Babalu-Aye', Ochosi, and Osain), plus deities of **ORIENTAL MYSTERY RELIGIONS** and

IMPERIAL ROMAN CULTS (Attis, Cybele, El-Gabal, Mithras, Sol Invictus, and Endovelicus), and the **URARTIAN GOD** Haldi, and you already have a rather UNWIELDY GAME OF CLUE on your hands! But then, refer to https://en.wikipedia.org/wiki/List_of_Celtic_deities for a list of nearly 300 additional **CELTIC DEITIES**! Finally, go to http://www.godchecker.com/pantheon/chinese-mythology.php?list-gods-names for a list of nearly 500 additional **CHINESE DEITIES**! It is unnecessary to say that our list in this chapter is illustrative, but still not exhaustive.

Fortunately, for the Whodunnit question concerning the creation of the universe, we can pare down our list of substantial "god suspects" by eliminating those who are not mentioned as involved in creation or universe formation. The God of logic as we have previously argued is a God of creative logic. Only a "creator god" will fit the description. On page 50 of my book *Disneology: Religious Rhetoric at Walt Disney World*, I point out:

> Virtually **EVERY ANCIENT CULTURE** offered explanations of our origins. The **EGYPTIANS** focused on the role of the *Nile River* in creation. They saw the beginning as a mass of *chaotic waters*, called *Nu* or *Nun*. To this beginning they added *Sun, Moon, Earth, and Sky gods*. The (immortal, but not eternal) Earth god and sky goddess eventually gave birth to *Isis* and *Osiris*, names better known to our generation, but Egyptian mythology (with such features as the Earth god lying on his side to form mountains) did not survive as a serious explanation of the beginnings of the world. According to an account of **PHOENICIAN** creation mythology dating at least as far back as the first century a.d., there was first *chaos*; then from a *cosmic egg*, creation of the universe began. **MAYAN** creation stories begin with *sky and sea*, and then the creation god *Kukulkan* (whose pyramid, incidentally, may be seen at the Mexico Pavilion in EPCOT) speaks the word

'Earth,' and the *Earth* rises from the sea. Following this, the *thoughts* of Kukulkan create *mountains*, *trees*, *birds*, *jaguars*, and *snakes*; finally, *humans* are created (first, out of *mud*; second, out of *wood*; third, as *monkeys*; and finally, as *full-fledged humans*). Vying with **GENESIS** as the oldest creation account is the **BABYLONIAN** creation myth. The Babylonian account we have is developed from **SUMERIAN** myths, in the 12th century b.c. According to this account, *god/s did not exist at the beginning* of the universe. Instead, *sweet and bitter waters comingled* and created many gods. Then, one god born of two others, *Marduk*, eventually defeated and killed the bitter waters, *Tiamat*, in a colossal struggle. *Earth* was created, followed by the *moon*, then the *Sun*. Finally, *humans* descended from the gods. **GREEK** creation mythology began with *chaos*, a watery state ruled by *Oceanus*, and as in the Babylonian account, *reproductive activity on the part of the gods and goddesses* produced the Greek gods. *Poseidon*, one of the great Greek gods (known by the **ROMANS** as *Neptune*), is featured in a fountain statue in the Italy exhibit in the 'World Showcase' at EPCOT.

We may further reduce the number of possible "god suspects" who could be the God of Logic if we assume that the God who created the universe in a logical (LOGOS) fashion, and who is characterized by the ability to communicate (LOGOS), and who fashioned human beings with the capacity for using both types of LOGOS, and presumably, was therefore willing and motivated to communicate with them through LOGOS, would be a God who made himself or herself known to ancient cultures *and would still be known to **contemporary** cultures*. We may, therefore eliminate virtually all the aforementioned gods and religions as "dead religions." Turning then, only to **CONTEMPORARILY VIABLE GODS**, we may consider the following list:

SHINTOISM and the **JAPANESE GODS**:   Amaterasu, Susanoo, Tsukiyomi, Inari, Tengu, Izanami, Izanagi, The Shichifukujin, Daikoku, Ebisu, Benzaiten, Bishamonten, Fukurokuju, Jurojin, and Hotei. Shintoism is a modern-day religion for an estimated four million Japanese, but most Japanese only identify as Shintoist while not practicing any religious discipline in the religion. In China, **BUDDHISM**, while it is a spiritual exercise, is not considered to have any true "god" associated with it. **HINDUISM**, according to https://en.wikipedia.org/wiki/Hindu_deities, is the "dominant religion of the Indian subcontinent." It has no specified number of gods, but is popularly credited with having 330 million gods. To this list of ancient-but-contemporarily-viable-gods, it is necessary to add the **ONE SINGLE GOD** who is acknowledged as God by the world's three major world religions—**JUDAISM, CHRISTIANITY,** and **ISLAM**.   That one God recognized by all three of these religions is the God of Abraham.

From this list, we may eliminate Buddhism, since it has no "god" associated with it. We may eliminate Shintoism, since it now appears to be primarily just a cultural practice, not a strongly held religion. If the God of Logic (LOGOS) is defined as organizing all the universe "logically," we may also eliminate Hinduism, which seems to be a hodge-podge of deities from other cultures and individual preferences. Logically, then, we conclude—along with the world's three greatest religions--that the God of Logic IS the God of Abraham.

Whodunnit? Similar to solving the Game of Clue—that Colonel Mustard killed Mr. Boddy in the Kitchen with the Knife—we may conclude logically that "the God of Abraham created a Logical

Universe and Logical Humans within that Logical Universe by means of the Agency of Communication/Spoken Word/LOGOS. If this is our conclusion, the next question becomes: "Which of the three major world religions best introduces us to the God of Abraham?" We'll consider that in the next chapter.

Chapter 7

SCANDALIZED: Paris 2015--Was Abraham a Killer?

Which of the top three world religions best represents the God of Abraham? As I was in the process of writing this chapter, at least 129 innocent people were being executed in Paris, in the name of the God of Abraham. Shouting "Allahu Akbar!" eight Muslim extremists, in a coordinated attack, bombed and shot Parisians and tourists who variously were dining, enjoying a concert, and attending a sporting event. Were these 129 victims soldiers who had attacked Islam? No. Were they particularly guilty of some heinous sin or crime? No. Just like the 3000 victims of the 9-11 Muslim extremist terrorist attacks in the United States, they were innocent bystanders. Shortly before the Paris attack, a Russian plane, returning 224 vacationers from Sharm el-Sheikh, Egypt were possibly bombed out of the sky. These passengers were, again, innocent bystanders, despite the fact that the Russian military itself had entered into armed conflict in Syria. The "Islamic State" claimed responsibility for these deaths.   What sort of religion encourages, celebrates, approves of, or even quietly condones the killing of innocents? The Hebrew word for Hell is Gē Hinnom (the Valley of Hinnom), the name of an area outside of Jerusalem where apostate Israelites had sacrificed their innocent children to the false god Molech. Due to this SCANDALOUS practice of killing children, Gē Hinnom became a name that forever after was considered cursed. Hell in both Judaism and Christianity is referred to as the Valley of Hinnom (Gehenna, in the Greek New Testament). So detestable was the thought of killing innocent children! I observe in my book *Psychotic Entelechy: The Dangers of Spiritual Gifts Theology:*

> Like Judaism and Christianity, Mohammed proclaimed the God of Abraham the true God and opposed sins such as murder and adultery. Like Christianity, Mohammed proclaimed Jesus the Messiah, the son of the virgin Mary. . . . Like the Catholic Church and many conservative Protestant churches, Islam opposes the practice of abortion (p.3).

A few pages later in the same book, I comment: "Darwinistic views devalued the lives of members of some races and the victims of some illnesses. Amoral pragmatic philosophies have paved the way for abortion and the infanticide of baby girls in Communist China" (p. 8). In the second decade of the Twenty-First Century, Americans were SCANDALIZED by the revelation of Planned Parenthood officials and doctors who had allegedly been harvesting fetuses and aborted baby parts for sale and profit. It is SCANDALOUS to kill these innocent unborn children, in the first place, but even more SCANDALOUS to attempt to profit from this butchery. On pages 72-79 of *Psychotic Entelechy*, I analyze the abortion debate from most major philosophic perspectives. On page 76, I observe:

Roman Catholicism, Islam, Evangelical Protestants, and some Jewish groups sense danger in the materialist, naturalist, and humanist abortion entelechies. Sheler [in *U. S. News and World Report* March 9, 1992, page 54] observes: "[T]he Roman Catholic Church and Evangelical Protestants have been highly visible in opposing abortion." The Islamic world has also been a strong opponent of abortion on a global scale as have Orthodox Jews. Without a strong alliance between Islam and the Catholic Church, abortion would be much more rampant world-wide than it currently is. Discussing basic Jewish and Christian morality, a very early Christian text, the *Didache*, states: "*Thou shalt do no* murder . . . thou shalt not murder a child by abortion nor kill them when born."

If Islam opposes the SCANDALOUS killing of innocent unborn children through abortion, what is it in the Islamic religion that would make Islamic extremists believe the God of Abraham would approve of them spilling the innocent blood in Paris on Friday the 13th of November 2015 or the innocent blood in the United States on 9/11/2001? We need only to consider the actions of Abraham--the common spiritual ancestor of Christianity, Islam, and Judaism—to catch a glimpse of the God of Abraham.

The year was 1967--the year I graduated from Easton High School, in Easton, IL. The movie "The Bible...In the Beginning" had been released in the preceding year, but it had just now arrived at my local theater. It was directed by the famous film director John Huston, who received 15 Oscar nominations and 2 actual Oscars during his film directing career. I supported the movie by buying tickets and attending the screening. I recall an incident that occurred while I was watching the movie in the theater. It clearly made an impression on me, since I have remembered the incident all these years!   George C. Scott, who portrayed Abraham in the film, was   (unbeknownst to his screen son, Isaac) taking Isaac up Mount Moriah (the mountain later to become the Temple Mount, in the days of King Solomon) because God had commanded him to sacrifice his son. Abraham required Isaac to carry the wood for the burnt offering, just as Jesus (2000 years later) was required to carry the wooden cross upon which he was to be crucified. Abraham bound Isaac and laid him upon the wood to which he would soon set fire, to offer Isaac as a burnt offering. Some audience members sitting in the row behind me at the theater were aghast! They were SCANDALIZED by the pending event. I heard them saying to one another statements such as: "How could any good God require such a thing!" "I can't believe in a God who would ask a man to kill his own son!" I realized that the audience members saying this were not familiar with the biblical account. I turned around and suggested, "Just keep watching. It's not going to end the way you think." In the biblical account (and the film), after Abraham had raised his knife to slay his son, the angel of God spoke to Abraham, telling him not to kill his son. God, instead, provided a ram, whose horns had been caught in the bushes, for Abraham to sacrifice, rather than to kill his only son. God was pleased with Abraham's willingness to sacrifice his son, however—despite the fact that God would not actually ask him to do such a thing. For any Jew (as it was for those sitting behind me at the movie theater), human sacrifice was SCANDALOUS!

The New Testament agrees with the account as described in the Old Testament (Hebrews 11:17 and James 2:21). While the Koran does not state explicitly that it was Isaac who was about to be sacrificed by Abraham, it does agree that Abraham was willing to sacrifice his son: "'O my son! I have seen in a vision that I offer thee in sacrifice: now see what is thy view!' (The son) said: 'O my father! Do as thou art commanded: thou will find me, if Allah so wills, one of the steadfast!'" (37:102)   While Muhammad Ghoniem & M S M Saifullah (http://www.islamic-awareness.org/Quran/Contrad/MusTrad/sacrifice.html) provide the argument that, even in the Koran, the son to whom Abraham was speaking in the Koranic account was actually Isaac, the much more common tradition among Muslims is that the son to be sacrificed was Ishmael, Abraham's son through Sarah's handmaid, Hagar. Ishmael is considered a prophet in Islam and is thought to be a progenitor of Mohammed. The Koranic account does not include the biblical detail that the sacrificial victim was to be replaced with a ram, but it suggests that Abraham's son is to be replaced with a "great sacrifice (*Zibhin azeem*)." I agree with Mohammed's assessment that God would be replacing Abraham's son with a great sacrifice, but who/what is this "great sacrifice"? How did the story of God commanding Abraham to commit human sacrifice (even if subsequently rescinded) become so significant in the religions of Israel, Islam, and Christianity? If the God of Abraham is the one who made the universe and creates and sustains all life, how can He ask someone to kill another innocent human being, let alone his own son? This seems SCANDALOUS! What is the significance of this Abrahamic sacrificial command?

In the previous chapter, I presented the logical argument that the God who created and animates the universe in logical fashion (and whose own nature as a logical communicator argues consistently with the assertion that He) is the God of Abraham. This is the conclusion of the world's three largest religions, but the question now arises: Which of these three religions best represents this God of Abraham?

JUDAISM correctly makes the claim that it is the OLDEST of the three religions. There is certainly some validity to the argument that, as the first religion to identify the God of Abraham as the one true God, Judaism's representation of that God deserves our attention. My master's degree (in Hebrew) was taken at the feet of an internationally-respected Jewish scholar at Indiana University: Dr. Henry A. Fischel. I gained a great deal of insight concerning the God of Abraham from my Hebrew and Aramaic language studies of the Old Testament and the Jewish literature that was produced after the Old Testament period—in times much closer to New Testament times. My master's thesis, *Anamartetous fallen angels*, which served as the basis for my book, entitled *Angels and demons: The personification of communication*, supplies many insights into the nature of the God of Abraham derived from primarily Jewish/Hebrew sources. That master's thesis was approved in writing not only by Dr. Fischel, but also by Christian scholar Dr. Paul Sampley and Islamic scholar Dr. Wadie Jwaideh. As it turns out, there is considerable agreement among the three religions in terms of angelology and other theological matters. Indeed, Christianity does not challenge the Jewish assertion that the Hebrew scriptures, which the Jews refer to as Tanach and the Christians refer to as the Old Testament, are supremely reliable accounts of the interactions of the God of Abraham with the Jewish people (in addition to various individuals living prior to the formation of the Jewish culture). Islam's holy scriptures, the Koran (or Qur'an), likewise pay homage to both Christians and Jews as being "people of the Book" (presumably, alluding to the essential genuineness of the Christian and Hebrew scriptures). While Christians and Jews are in general agreement regarding the make-up and reliability of the Old Testament/Tanach, Muslims are less-enthusiastically supportive, suggesting that certain passages in the Old Testament ("the Book," as the Koran refers to it) have become corrupted, over the years. On page 70 of *Psychotic Entelechy*, I phrase it this way: "Christians and Jews do not believe that the Koran is a collection of divine revelations, just as 'Muslims believe that . . . Jewish and Christian scriptures have been corrupted and are no longer reliable, or are superseded by the Qur'an, and hence no longer necessary.'" Thus, most Muslims claim that it was Ishmael, rather than Isaac, who was the object of Abraham's intended sacrifice.

From the time of Moses, the principle of killing a lamb as a substitute for losing the life of a child is reinforced. Rather than have the death angel take the lives of the first-born males of the Israelites as happened in the final plague upon Egypt, God told the Israelites to kill a lamb and smear its blood on each doorpost. The death angel would then "Pass Over" the household, leaving the first-born Israelite male from that family alive. To this day, Jews celebrate the Passover feast.

Why do Christians and Muslims not simply accede to the superiority of Judaism as the best representation of the God of Abraham? From CHRISTIANITY'S perspective, the Hebrew Scriptures were incomplete. That is, a sizeable portion of these scriptures pointed to a future revelation of the God of Abraham in history. Jews, to this very day, understand that their scriptures promised the coming of a MESSIAH (Hebrew) or CHRIST (Greek). Islam is not the only one of the three religions that sensed that the killing of a ram was not a sufficient substitute for the sacrifice of Abraham's son. Not only does the Koran suggest that Abraham's son is to be replaced with a "great sacrifice," even the Hebrew Scriptures recognize the ineffectiveness of animal sacrifices. David, in Psalm 69:31 suggests that God prefers songs of praise to the sacrifice of animals.   Isaiah 1:11 states: "The multitude of your sacrifices-- what are they to me?" says the LORD. "I have more than enough of burnt offerings, of rams and the fat of fattened animals; I have no pleasure in the blood of bulls and lambs and goats" (NIV). In a passage taken by the New Testament to be a prophecy concerning Jesus' crucifixion, Isaiah 59:3-7 states:

> 3He was despised and rejected by mankind, a man of suffering, and familiar with pain. Like one from whom people hide their faces, he was despised, and we held him in low esteem. 4Surely he took up our pain and bore our suffering, yet we considered him punished by God, stricken by him, and afflicted. 5But he was pierced for our transgressions, he was crushed for our iniquities; the punishment that brought us peace was on him, and by his wounds we are healed. 6We all, like sheep, have gone astray, each of us has turned to our own way; and the LORD has laid on him the iniquity of us all. 7He was oppressed and afflicted, yet he did not open his mouth; he was led like a lamb to the slaughter, and as a sheep before its shearers is silent, so he did not open his mouth (NIV).

The Gospel of John describes a moment in which the statements of Jesus SCANDALIZED many of his fellow Jews. The substance of Jesus' statements have to do with human sacrifice. This was considered SCANDALOUS by many of his countrymen.   John 6:48-66 records the SCANDALOUS comments:

> 48"I am the bread of life. 49Your ancestors ate the manna in the wilderness, yet they died. 50But here is the bread that comes down from heaven, which anyone may eat and not die. 51I am the living bread that came down from heaven. Whoever eats this bread will live forever. This bread is my flesh, which I will give for the life of the world." 52Then the Jews began to argue sharply among themselves, "How can this man give us his flesh to eat?" 53Jesus said to them, "Very truly I tell

you, unless you eat the flesh of the Son of Man and drink his blood, you have no life in you. 54Whoever eats my flesh and drinks my blood has eternal life, and I will raise them up at the last day. 55For my flesh is real food and my blood is real drink. 56Whoever eats my flesh and drinks my blood remains in me, and I in them. 57Just as the living Father sent me and I live because of the Father, so the one who feeds on me will live because of me . . . " 60On hearing it, many of his disciples said, "This is a hard teaching. Who can accept it?" 61Aware that his disciples were grumbling about this, Jesus said to them, "Does this offend you? . . . 66From this time many of his disciples turned back and no longer followed him" (NIV).

While some commentators suggest that what SCANDALIZED the crowds was a claim to be divine on Jesus' part, I think that, clearly, the SCANDALOUS nature of this account is that it proposes a human sacrifice. Just as Isaac had just turned 13 years of age at the time of Abraham's test (and, hence, was considered "innocent" by Jewish culture, having just then arrived at the age for Bar Mitzvah—the age of accountability), Jesus, as it is contended by Christians was also "innocent." He had lived more than 30 years—but was not guilty of any sin. Therefore, Jesus would qualify as an appropriate substitute for Isaac. He was offering himself as a HUMAN SACRIFICE. That was the part that was SCANDALOUS. Just as Jews had, for years, consumed the meat of the animal sacrifice they had offered for their sins, Jesus SCANDALIZED his countrymen by inviting them to consume his flesh and blood. No human in history has ever actually eaten Jesus' flesh, nor had any of his disciples in the time John wrote his account. Therefore, John could not have understood Jesus' words to be taken strictly literally.

(Actually, Catholics come close to taking his words literally, in their doctrine of Transubstantiation. They posit that the bread and wine of Communion literally are transubstantiated into Jesus' actual flesh and blood at the moment they are consumed in the Eucharist. However, the Catholic Church fails to take into account the fact that the Gospel of John, in which this account occurs, is the ONLY ONE OF THE FOUR GOSPELS that does NOT present Jesus as instituting the Lord's Supper! More on this point, momentarily.)

Yet, in a definite sense, Jesus' words were to be taken literally! Jesus was literally going to become a human sacrifice. His blood was literally going to be poured out. His flesh was literally going to be killed. Like Isaac, he literally carried the wood on which he would be killed to the mountain. There is no Abrahamic substitute of a ram for his son, here—even though Jesus was quite literally a "son of Abraham," as traced by the beginning of the genealogy of Jesus in Matthew 1:2, and confirmed in Luke 3:34. The major logical point John has been making throughout his gospel is that Jesus is the Lamb of God who takes away the sin of the world (John 1:29, 36). The reason John does not present Jesus as celebrating the Passover meal with his disciples and introducing the Lord's Supper, is because John is following a different Jewish calendar, according to which Jesus was killed at precisely the time Jews kill the Passover Lamb. He could not, therefore, eat the Passover meal (according to John's calendar), because he was dead by the time it would have been consumed (the evening after it was killed). There is no substitute of a Passover Lamb, here; Jesus IS LITERALLY THE HUMAN PASSOVER LAMB. But, unlike the animal sacrifices which had no free will to offer their lives and unlike even Isaac who was bound by Abraham, and therefore coerced into becoming a potential sacrifice, Jesus VOLUNTARILY offered his own body and blood to be sacrificed. No one took his life; he gave it freely. John 10:18 presents Jesus' words: "[18] No one takes it from me, but I lay it down of my own accord. I have authority to lay it down and authority to take it up again" (NIV).

This is the logic of Christianity. It meets the Koranic suggestion that Abraham's son is to be replaced with a "great sacrifice." It encompasses Isaiah's view that God has "no pleasure in the blood of bulls and lambs and goats." It further presents Jesus as Isaiah's suffering servant who was led to the slaughter like a lamb. It explains logically Isaiah's thesis that "he was pierced for our transgressions, he was crushed for our iniquities; the punishment that brought us peace was on him, and by his wounds we are healed." In my next chapter, I will discuss the logic of why Jesus' sacrifice was the perfect substitutionary sacrifice.

Chapter 8

The Missing Link: The Transfiguration

It is described in detail in three of the four gospels, the book of Second Peter, and, as I argue, in what even many liberal scholars consider to be the earliest Christian doctrinal statement in the New Testament (the "Philippians Hymn" in Paul's writings). Yet, it does not get the respect it deserves, in the Logic of Christianity: The TRANSFIGURATION. Scholars have seen the parallel between Jesus' baptism and His transfiguration. In both instances, a voice from heaven (which Jews call a Bat Qol) states: "This is my beloved Son, in whom I am well-pleased." Certainly, Jesus' BAPTISM is a pillar of the logic of Christianity, since it is described in three of the four gospels, even though it is not mentioned in Paul's writings or any other New Testament book. Along with the CRUCIFIXION and the RESURRECTION, which are found or alluded to in virtually every part of the New Testament, and the ASCENSION, which is described in detail in Luke, Acts, Revelation, and Mark, and certainly assumed in Paul's writings and the rest of the

New Testament, these events are the pillars of the Logic of Christianity. So, why is the Transfiguration discussed so little among Christian theologians and biblical scholars? It's a difficult issue to grasp.

WHAT IS ITS SIGNIFICANCE?

I will present, in this chapter, an explanation of the Transfiguration that can remove the confusion over why it was essential to the Logic of Christianity THAT JESUS BE THE ONE WHO OFFERS HIMSELF AS A SACRIFICE for the sins of Adam and all of Adam's progeny. Incorrectly, I think, on various websites (such as http://www.gotquestions.org/transfiguration.html), it is suggested that the point of the Transfiguration was to demonstrate the DEITY of Jesus to his disciples. Symbolically, these websites also suggest that Moses represents the Law and Elijah the prophets (following Origen, who was the first to make the connection and Luther, who agreed), so when the voice from heaven says to "listen to" His Son, it means that Jesus is more important than the Law and the Prophets. ALSO, for the most part INCORRECTLY, Gospels scholar Charles H. Talbert presents the transfiguration accounts as Jesus' disciples seeing Jesus—as something of a PREVIEW, in a dream vision—that predicted how Jesus would appear, at a LATER date, at his PAROUSIA (Talbert, *Matthew*, 203-204). While I do not accept Talbert's dream vision explanation, to his credit Talbert (206) points to the following fact:

> Jewish apocalyptic expectation that MOSES AND ELIJAH would come together
> as part of the eschatological windup of history (e.g., Deut. Rab. 3.17 on Deut. 10:1:
> a saying attributed to Rabbi Johanan ben Zachai; Rev. 11:3-6; . . . MOSES was
> regarded by some Jews as one who was taken up, as were ELIJAH AND ENOCH,

cf. Josephus, Ant. 4:323-26; Sifre 357 on Deut. 34:5; Clement of Alexandria Strom. 6.15.132; Joshua saw Moses ascend with the angel, Jerome, Comm. Amos 9.6; MOSES ASCENDS LIKE ENOCH AND ELIJAH)."

It is this connection with Elijah, [Enoch,] And Moses that makes the transfiguration logically foundational.

Talbert regards the 2 Peter 1:16-18 passage as a proof that the Transfiguration was understood to primarily signify a preview of Jesus' power and coming (PAROUSIA), but this passage certainly would not support Talbert's position that this was a dream vision. The very "proof" being offered in this passage is that the writer was an "eyewitness" who actually "heard" the voice from heaven" when he was actually "on the mountain." This passage is considered by the author of Second Peter to be proof that the disciples were not following "cleverly devised stories." They personally witnessed the event.

Furthermore, Talbert's "dream vision" interpretation overlooks a key PROOF CATEGORY for Jews at the time of Jesus—BAT QOL (or Voice from Heaven). For Jews of that era, the time of "prophecy" had ceased with the last book of the Tanach (Old Testament). The only ways that God still spoke freshly to humans, for Rabbinic Judaism, were through children, fools, and BAT QOL (or mysterious voice from Heaven). Jesus alludes to the proofs of God speaking through children during his Palm Sunday entry into Jerusalem (Matthew 21:15-16). And, while Christianity disagrees that the age of prophecy had ended (there are plenty of Christian prophecies), it certainly affords the proof that was still acceptable to Jews: BAT QOL. This mysterious voice occurs at

Jesus' baptism and at his transfiguration. Jesus, himself, voices the BAT QOL when he speaks to Saul of Tarsus on the road to Damascus.

In an earlier book, *What Is a Gospel*, Talbert seems to hint that the Transfiguration may just be a mythic element, along with the Ascension, that attempts to present Jesus as an "IMMORTAL." He defines immortals as "gods who had a beginning to their existence and had not existed eternally" (26). He mentions a Roman belief from just before the birth of Christ that Hercules and Asclepius "ascended to heaven and . . . obtained the same honors as the gods." To the mythology of Greek immortals "ascending," Talbert adds "transformation" (as in transfiguration) as a proof of immortality (27). He further states: "whenever Mediterranean peoples spoke about the immortals constant in their description was . . . 'he was taken up into heaven.'" This event was either "witnessed or there was no trace of physical remains." Further evidence of this transformation/ascension, according to Talbert, were "a heavenly announcement at the end of his earthly career" and "appearances . . . to friends or disciples." Additional evidence of being an immortal is "reference to the man's being begotten by a god of a human mother" (28).

Sure enough, according to Talbert's hints, the story of Jesus sounds very much like the story of an immortal. If the New Testament story supplies "proofs" such as the "words of children" and the "BAT QOL" that are persuasive to Jewish audiences, it also supplies "proofs" such as the "proofs of immortality" that are persuasive to Greek audiences (and even "astrological" proofs such as the star of Bethlehem that are persuasive to Magi). But, did the Greeks invent the category of "immortals," themselves, or did they somehow receive it from much older accounts, such as (Hebrew) scriptures?

THE CASE OF ENOCH

In the fifth chapter of the very first book in the Bible, Genesis 5:22-24 records this account:

> [22]And Enoch walked with God after he begat Methuselah three hundred years, and begat sons and daughters: [23]And all the days of Enoch were three hundred sixty and five years: [24]And Enoch walked with God: and he [was] not; for God took him (KJV).

The New Testament book of Hebrews (11:5) interprets this passage as a statement that Enoch became an immortal: "By faith Enoch was taken from this life, so that he did not experience death: 'He could not be found, because God had taken him away.' For before he was taken, he was commended as one who pleased God" (NIV). Although it was doubtlessly influenced by Greek mythology, the *Book of Enoch*, written in Greek (AND CLEARLY NOT BY ENOCH HIMSELF!), between 300 and 1 B.C., presents Enoch as having become an immortal, but neither the *Book of Enoch* nor the book of Hebrews offers any claim (in any way similar to Talbert's definition of a Greek immortal) that Enoch became a "god." Nevertheless, the case of Enoch is the first Hebrew example of a human who appears to have achieved immortality without dying. While I wonder why Enoch was not included in the Transfiguration event, along with Jesus, Moses, and Elijah, the answer could pertain to the fact that Enoch was from generations prior to Abraham, Isaac, and Israel, while Moses, Elijah, and Jesus were Israelites. Another explanation for the absence of Enoch might be that the *Book of Enoch* had become such a discredited book by the New Testament period that even Enoch himself was rarely mentioned, which point I make in my book *Angels and demons: The personification of communication* (Chapter 13: "Who are the 'Sons of God' in Genesis"):

> Louis Ginzberg notes that all of the Enoch legends "left no trace in the authoritative rabbinic sources," and Bamberger goes so far as to say that Enoch "is not mentioned at all" in "the two Talmuds and in the tannaitic literature." Bamberger does admit, in the footnotes (p. 275), that "actually Enoch is mentioned (but just mentioned)" in Seder Olam Rabbah, chapter 1, beginning. Then, two or three more references in the standard midrashim round out the references to Enoch. One of those references (Bereshit Rabbah 25.1) mentions Enoch, but only to claim that he was NOT translated to Heaven. Other than the reference to Enoch in Jude 14 and the few allusions to I Enoch in Jude, the only reference to Enoch in the New Testament is Hebrews 11:5, which merely lists Enoch as an example of faith who did not die.

THE CASE OF MOSES

The Bible never states that Moses was transfigured, translated, or transported from Earth to Heaven in a fiery chariot. While there are other non-biblical texts (cited by Talbert earlier in this chapter) that suggest that Moses ascended and/or went to Heaven, without dying, in a fashion similar to Enoch and Elijah, this was a hotly debated point, even at the time of the New Testament, among Jews. The gospel accounts of the Transfiguration do not suggest how Moses managed to accompany Elijah to the mountain. Nevertheless, the biblical account of Moses' "death" in Deuteronomy seems pregnant with possibilities:

> 34 Then Moses climbed Mount Nebo from the plains of Moab to the top of Pisgah, across from Jericho. There the LORD showed him the whole land—from

Gilead to Dan, [2] all of Naphtali, the territory of Ephraim and Manasseh, all the land of Judah as far as the Mediterranean Sea, [3] the Negev and the whole region from the Valley of Jericho, the City of Palms, as far as Zoar. [4] Then the LORD said to him, "This is the land I promised on oath to Abraham, Isaac and Jacob when I said, 'I will give it to your descendants.' I have let you see it with your eyes, but you will not cross over into it."

[5] And Moses the servant of the LORD died there in Moab, as the LORD had said. [6] He buried him[a] in Moab, in the valley opposite Beth Peor, BUT TO THIS DAY NO ONE KNOWS WHERE HIS GRAVE IS (NIV, emphasis mine).

Verses 5 and 6 are the curious ones. Prior to these two verses, there is no mention of Moses dying. Furthermore, the verses speak of Moses in third person and clearly cannot have been written by Moses, even if they correctly recorded his death and burial. No eye witness of this event is, however, mentioned in the Deuteronomy text. This point was not lost on Jewish readers, since the book of Deuteronomy is traditionally assigned Mosaic authorship. How can Moses record his own death and burial? And, if Moses DID record it (in past tense), does that then indicate that Moses was alive again after his death and burial, and thus able to record it? On top of these questions, Greeks who are aware of the "proofs" of immortality to which Talbert referred earlier will find the phrasing of verse 6—"And he buried him in a valley in the land of Moab, over against Bethpeor: but no man knoweth of his sepulchre unto this day" (KJV)—strongly suggestive of immortals mythology. Talbert suggests that an immortalizing event was either "witnessed or there was no trace of physical remains." There were no witnesses to Moses' death (that we know of) and no trace of his sepulchre. If Moses is understood to have literally died and been buried, something strange has reportedly occurred. Moses is on the mountain WITH ELIJAH, according to gospel accounts. Was there a rapid-fire resurrection event for Moses? Did he still have the same body or was his body an immortal body as he appeared on the mountain?

THE CASE OF ELIJAH

If it is argued that the Genesis account of Enoch is too brief to be certain that it was an immortalizing event, and if the Deuteronomy account of Moses' death is too confusing to reach any conclusions, still the account of Elijah being taken to Heaven in a fiery chariot is much more conclusive evidence of a Jewish teaching of an immortalizing event. All three cases (Enoch, Moses, and Elijah) were recorded long before Greek mythology became an important factor in Jewish scripture and lore. Elijah was from the 8th century B.C., Moses was from the 16th century B.C., and Enoch was, according to Jude, the 7th generation after Adam. Alexander the Great's Greek Empire which reached to the Middle East did not occur until the 4th century B.C. 2 Kings, chapter 2, records the event:

> 2 When the LORD was about to take Elijah up to heaven in a whirlwind, Elijah and Elisha were on their way from Gilgal. ² Elijah said to Elisha, "Stay here; the LORD has sent me to Bethel."
>
> But Elisha said, "As surely as the LORD lives and as you live, I will not leave you." So they went down to Bethel. . . .
>
> ¹¹ As they were walking along and talking together, suddenly a chariot of fire and horses of fire appeared and separated the two of them, and Elijah went up to

heaven in a whirlwind. [12] Elisha saw this and cried out, "My father! My father! The chariots and horsemen of Israel!" And Elisha saw him no more. (NIV)

THE CASE OF JESUS

The syllogism looks like this:

> MAJOR PREMISE: The wages of sin is death (Romans 6:23—This is backed up by the first sin of Adam and Eve and their punishment for that sin: death.)
>
> MINOR PREMISE: Elijah (and Enoch?) did not die.
>
> CONCLUSION: Elijah (and Enoch?) did not sin.

If, then, Jesus is on a mountaintop with Elijah (and Moses), toward the end of his earthly life, and suddenly finds his own body metamorphosing into something of brilliance, one must assume that Jesus has accomplished the same feat as Elijah—living his life without sinning! Just as Moses was on a mountain for his departure, Jesus was on a mountain. Just as there was a fiery brilliance at Elijah's departure, brilliant light and shining countenance were signs of what was happening to Jesus. JESUS WAS BECOMING IMMORTAL. He, like Elijah (and Enoch—and, possibly, Moses) had ACTUALLY EARNED ETERNAL LIFE. He didn't accomplish this feat in the way Greeks purportedly became immortals; he accomplished it through piety. Jewish scholars have noted that, at the time Abraham was asked to sacrifice Isaac, Isaac had just reached the age of accountability. In the Hebrew, he is called a Na'ar. It means he has just reached the age for his bar-Mitzvah. From now on in his life, he must follow the Commandments. He is considered innocent, at this point. Therefore, Isaac might have made a good sacrifice for the sins of Adam and his progeny, but God said "No." (The Jewish rabbis told a story of a young female equivalent to a Na'ar—the feminine is Na'arah—who was tested by angels to sin, and who successfully passed her test and went straight to Heaven. I relate this story in my book *Angels and demons: The personification of communication* (Chapter 6: An 'Innocent' Fallen Angel Story"). The principle is clear in Jewish logic: One who has not sinned is capable of being translated to Heaven. Nevertheless, someone who has just reached the age of accountability—or even an innocent infant—is not an acceptable sacrifice for the sin of Adam. It takes someone who has lived a significant lifetime, yet who did not sin. Not many people qualify. The blood of bulls and goats is not sufficient to remove sin. The blood of infants and young people who have just begun to be tested is not sufficient to remove sin. It takes the blood of an immortal—one who has lived a significant lifetime (sinlessly) to serve as the perfect sacrifice. Enoch might have qualified, but he apparently took eternal life when it was offered. Maybe Moses, but especially Elijah, might have qualified, but they both apparently accepted immortality, when it was offered. Only Jesus, among biblical immortals—those who lived a significant lifetime, yet without sin—was willing and ready to relinquish the reward he had earned: eternal life.

This brings us to the Philippians Hymn, Philippians 2:5-11 (NIV):

> [5] In your relationships with one another, have the same mindset as Christ Jesus: [6] Who, being in very form God, did not consider equality with God something to be used to his own advantage; [7] rather, he made himself nothing by taking the very form of a servant, being made in human likeness. [8] And being found in appearance as a man, he humbled himself by becoming obedient to death—even death on a

cross! [9] Therefore God exalted him to the highest place and gave him the name that is above every name, [10] that at the name of Jesus every knee should bow, in heaven and on earth and under the earth, [11] and every tongue acknowledge that Jesus Christ is Lord, to the glory of God the Father."

Most Christians read this hymn from the interpretive perspective that the time when Jesus found himself in the "form" of God was some pre-existent period, before his birth, but the hymn never states that. I suggest that a more meaningful perspective would place this hymn in the context of Jesus' Transfiguration. He found himself in the "form" of God. The Greek word I have translated "form" in both verses 6 and 7 is the word MORPH, as in the word METAMORPHOSIS, the very word that is translated TRANSFIGURED in Matthew 17:2 and Mark 9:2, the Transfiguration accounts. Reading the Philippians Hymn from this interpretive perspective, we are encouraged to be SELFLESS, as Jesus was when he found himself transfigured into an immortal form. But, unlike Moses and Elijah, Jesus did not consider this immortal form something to be grasped, but returned to his earlier MORPH (that of a servant, a mortal), thus humbling himself and becoming obedient to death—EVEN THOUGH HE HAD PERSONALLY ACHIEVED IMMORTALITY! Furthermore, his death was not an ordinary death, or even the quick stabbing of a sacrificial animal. His death was the long, painful, excruciating death on a cross—the sentence of the very worst of criminals. And, therefore, because Jesus had paid the death penalty of even the worst criminals known to man, since he himself was worthy of immortality, the payment was not needed for his own account. It was applied to the account of EVERY SINGLE SINNING HUMAN FROM THE

TIME OF ADAM TO THE END OF THE WORLD. That's why God exalted him. That's why every knee bows. That's why every tongue confesses that Jesus is Lord, to the glory of God the Father!

Now, every great pillar of the Logic of Christianity has its own hymns or songs. There are Christmas songs celebrating the birth of Christ, like Joy to the World. There are baptismal songs. There are songs about the Last Supper. There are songs about the crucifixion on Calvary. There are Easter songs about the Resurrection and the Ascension. But, I'm hard-pressed to think of a strong doctrinal song about the Transfiguration. So, I wrote one and "published" a music video of it on YouTube. You may listen to it and view it at the following URL:

https://www.youtube.com/watch?v=LMuW4SeThlw&feature=youtu.be

Chapter 9

The Justice Link: The Crucifixion

DID JESUS RECEIVE JUSTICE? One of the three major genres of rhetoric, according to Aristotle, is JUDICIAL RHETORIC. Here, Aristotle asserts that LOGOS (or logic) is the major proof used to persuade a judge or jury that JUSTICE has been or will be enacted.

If the Transfiguration is the Missing Link in the Logic of Christianity, the Crucifixion and Resurrection combine to form the Key Links. The Transfiguration account is referred to in more parts of the New Testament than Jesus' birth, pre-existence, baptism, genealogy, Ascension, miracles, parables, healings, Great Commission, Last Supper, childhood, or even his mother Mary. His Lordship, Messiahship, and Twelve Apostles (although, often, only two of them by name) are mentioned in more parts of the New Testament than the Transfiguration, but these are not events (as is the Transfiguration). Only two historic events receive mention in more parts of the New

Testament than his Transfiguration: his Crucifixion and his Resurrection. In my next chapter, I will consider the key logical link of the Resurrection. This chapter, however, will focus on the key logical link related to the ISSUE OF JUSTICE: the CRUCIFIXION. This, then, is Judicial Rhetoric.

The term "crucify," along with its cognates, is mentioned in all four gospels, Acts, Hebrews, Revelation and four of Paul's letters (I and II Corinthians, Romans, and Colossians). An additional five letters of Paul (Galatians, Ephesians, Philippians, II Timothy, and I Thessalonians), plus I Peter, use a cognate of the term "die" to refer to Jesus' death. Another Pauline letter, I Timothy, speaks of Jesus before "Pontius Pilate." The book of James mentions the "killing" of Jesus. I John speaks of our redemption through the "blood" of Christ. Other (short) New Testament books just appear to take it for granted that Jesus died by crucifixion. No New Testament book appears, in any way, to dispute his Crucifixion. Even though we have not yet thoroughly established the logical link that the New Testament is fully inspired and trustworthy in every respect (which we will get to, in time), this textual evidence shows virtually unanimous support from the writers of the New Testament for the proposition that Jesus was indeed crucified. He died one of the cruelest deaths of any human. Jesus was mortal.

You may ask, "Why does this matter?" Well, to begin with, there were early heretics, according to Charles S. Clifton, who held that Jesus did not die. Clifton writes:

> particularly Gentile converts [who] refused to believe that Jesus had a mortal body,
> a position that has come to be known as Docetism . . . The Pagan gods . . . had
> occasionally appeared in mortal form and vanished when their purposes were

accomplished; with them there was no death and resurrection . . . To these Christians [heretics], who included many of the so-called Gnostics, the crucifixion was only a show, a hallucination projected to observers. It was unthinkable that a divine being could physically suffer and die (*Encyclopedia of Heresies and Heretics*, xii).

Clifton continues later:

> The reverse of Docetism might be said to be those explanations of the crucifixion that claim that Jesus himself was not crucified but died a normal death at some other time and place. Parts of the New Testament appear to have been written to counter Docetic teachings . . . [I John] 4:2-3 . . . says, "This is how we may recognize the Spirit of God: every spirit which acknowledges that Jesus Christ has come in the flesh is from God, and every spirit which does not thus acknowledge Jesus is not from God." Likewise, . . . [II John] says, "Many deceivers have gone out into the world, who do not acknowledge Jesus Christ as coming in the flesh . . . If anyone comes to you who does not bring this doctrine, do not welcome him into your house or give him a greeting; for anyone who gives him a greeting is an accomplice in his wicked deeds."

Following the Logic of the Transfiguration as I presented it in the previous chapter: Jesus, while personally earning eternal life by living a perfect life, refused to accept the immortal "form" (i.e., like "God's" immortal "form" [Philippians 2:6-8]) and returned to the "form" of a human/servant who was capable of death (being mortal). He was obedient to death—even the death of the cross. The Transfiguration was the ULTIMATE PROOF that Jesus was RIGHTEOUS. Jesus did not sin at any point in his life.

There are other INNOCENT humans who die, however. Couldn't the death of one of these other "innocents" have sufficed as a sacrifice? Babies, according to Jewish (Rabbinic) and Christian (New Testament) teachings are "innocent." In other words, THEY HAVE NO SIN CHARGED AGAINST THEM. Setting aside, for the moment, the Catholic doctrine of "original sin," which prompts the Catholic Church to baptize babies to secure forgiveness for their sins, the dominant Judeo-Christian view at the time of the New Testament was that babies were innocent. According to Rabbinic Judaism, it was necessary for an individual to have both the good and evil "inclinations" to be held accountable for sin (and for that matter, to be deemed righteous for passing the test/temptation). The rich young ruler, with whom Jesus interacts regarding eternal life in Luke 18:18-21, insists that he has kept the "commandments" from his "youth" up. It is certainly possible (even, probable) that he means from the time of his bar mitzvah forward. Hebrews 4:15 asserts that Jesus himself was tempted in every respect, as we are, but was without sin. We know nothing, however, about the childhood of Jesus. After the birth narratives, there is no discussion of Jesus' actions until we near his bar mitzvah. Luke picks up the narrative again, in 2:41, when Jesus was age twelve. Why was Jesus taken to Jerusalem when he was twelve? Why didn't Mary and Joseph wait until he was thirteen, the appropriate age for a bar mitzvah? The Mishnah supplies the answer in Yoma 8:4: "Young children [anyone just born through 13 years for boys and 12 years for girls] are not made to fast on Yom Kippur, but we should train them a year or two before [they reach age 13, for boys, 12 for girls], so that they become used to (the observance of) commandments." I encouraged my four children to be baptized immediately following the twelfth birthday of my daughters and the thirteenth birthday of my sons. As I

understand Jewish and New Testament teachings, they were innocent before those ages.

A second category of "innocent humans" who die follow the Isaac pattern. Isaac had just reached

the appropriate age for a bar mitzvah. Theoretically, he was still sinless, but was responsible for

any sin after that time. The same theology allows Jewish writers to tell a story of a "lass" [a young

girl age 12] being righteous in one temptation following her "youth" and being awarded eternal

life. Since the "lass" possessed only the "evil inclination" prior to her twelfth birthday, any selfish

behavior committed prior to this time must NOT have been considered "sinful." This is precisely

the view (the sinlessness of children) that prevailed at this time of the New Testament. Even the

second book of Maccabees 8:4 speaks of the "sinless infants." And the Mishnah (Yoma 8:4)

agrees, concerning the Day of Atonement (Yom Kippur). It is a simple deduction that, if little

children are not required to participate in the yearly atonement exercise, they must not be held

guilty of any "sins" for which they would need atonement. Jesus corroborates this view of sinless

children when he commands his disciples to "suffer the little children to come unto me, for of such

is the kingdom of Heaven" (Matt. 19:13-15; Mark 10:13-14; Luke 18:15-16;). In Mark 10:15

(KJV), Jesus elaborates: "Whoever does not receive the kingdom of God as a little child, he shall

in no wise enter therein." While many interpretations of this comment have been offered, it is

possible that he is saying that one must be innocent, as a little child is, to enter the kingdom of

God. Matthew's version of this comment (Matt. 18:1-6 [KJV]) puts it this way:

> In that hour came the disciples unto Jesus, saying, "Who then is greatest in the
>
> kingdom of heaven?" And he called to him a little child, and set him in the midst

of them, and said, "Verily I say unto you, except ye turn, and become as little children, ye shall in no wise enter into the kingdom of heaven. Whosoever therefore shall humble himself as this little child, the same is the greatest in the kingdom of heaven. And whoso shall receive one such child in my name receiveth me: But whoso shall cause one of these little ones that believe on me to stumble, it is profitable for him that a great millstone should be hanged about his neck, and that he should be sunk in the depth of the sea."

In Matthew 21:15-16 (KJV), Jesus comments on the fact that children were shouting, "Hosanna to the son of David," as Jesus entered Jerusalem on Palm Sunday. Jesus cites Psalm 8:2 (KJV), saying: "Did you never read 'Out of the mouths of babes and sucklings you have perfected praise'?" Alluding to Psalm 8:2 (KJV)—"Out of the mouth of babes and sucklings has thou established strength"—Jesus appears to be confirming a point I made in my previous chapter on the Transfiguration: "The only ways that God still spoke freshly to humans, for Rabbinic Judaism, were through children, fools, and the BAT QOL (or mysterious voice from Heaven)." It seems that both children and fools were considered innocent, because they lack the good inclination. Therefore, the Holy Spirit (which inspires prophecy) is able to dwell inside these humans—they are innocent—in the same logical move that prompted Acts 2:17-18 to report that (after Jesus' death and resurrection) "the Spirit" could be "poured out" on all flesh. Once Jesus' death provided the forgiveness, the "NOW innocent" believers could receive the Holy Spirit.

Apparently, the death of neither children nor those who remain innocent for a short while following their bar mitzvah or bat mitzvah will suffice as an appropriate sacrifice for the sins of the world. Otherwise, Isaac would have been an appropriate sacrifice.

So, we come to Jesus of Nazareth. Of what sin was Jesus guilty? A few charges were floated:

1. "Sedition" against the Roman Empire (the official charge pertaining to his crucifixion),

2. Violating the Sabbath (by healing and harvesting grain; hence, working on the Sabbath),

3. Blasphemy, and

4. Not showing proper respect to the High Priest

SEDITION

While no term for "sedition" (STASIS, DICHOSTASIA, OR STASIAZO) is ever used to charge Jesus for a crime in the New Testament, one or another of these terms is applied variously to Barabbas, Paul, the Pharisees and Sadducees, and others. Paul is accused by his Jewish opponents of fomenting sedition against Rome, but he is never actually accused of taking up arms against Rome, as is Barabbas. Yet, the sign that hung above Jesus on the cross stated "King of the Jews" in three different languages. Clearly, the justification that Rome used for killing Jesus was that he was leading a revolt against Rome. Yet, Jesus rebuked Peter for drawing his sword and severing the ear of a guard who came to arrest Jesus. Jesus healed the wound. Indeed, to the frustration of modern-day Christians who surely see in the Old Testament their right to use weapons, and even kill, in self-defense (Exodus 22:2) and who see Moses killing an Egyptian to defend an Israelite, the behavior and teachings of the Prince of Peace were totally non-violent. Never mind that even Abraham led his household and others in war against the invaders from Mesopotamia who attacked his nephew, Lot, and rescued him from their grasp. For this act of war, Melchizedek "blessed" Abraham and Abraham paid Melchizedek a tithe from the booty. Yet, Jesus was not even a self-defense war monger (although he did permit his disciples to be armed with swords, apparently). Jesus told his followers to "love their enemies," to "turn the other cheek." No reputable evidence exists that Jesus was fomenting sedition against Rome. To the contrary, when Jesus was confronted by his enemies with the "gotcha" question, "Is it lawful to pay taxes to Caesar?"—an attempt to prove that Jesus was seditious because he would oppose paying the required tax to Rome—he asks for a coin, observes that the "image" on the coin is of Caesar, and probably alluding to the fact that man is made in the "image" of God—he ingeniously replies: "Render to Caesar the things that are Caesar's and unto God the things that are God's" (Matt. 22:21; Mark 12:17 [KJV]). Translation: Give your money (with Caesar's image) to Caesar, but your life and body (with God's image) to God. There is no sign of Jesus mounting a revolt against Rome. Even though he readily confessed to Pilate that he was a "king," he quickly stipulates that his kingdom is not of this world. Jesus was not seditious. But, even if he were mounting a revolt against Rome, that would not have been a SIN! Jesus is not guilty of a sin, here.

BLASPHEMY

Even James Still, who writes a blog hostile to Christianity in which he argues that Jesus was politically seditious against Rome admits:

It was not blasphemous to declare oneself a 'Messiah' or a 'Son of God' any more than it would have been to claim to be an angel. The Pharisees who composed the majority of the Sanhredrin would dismiss such a charge at once since blasphemy could only be applied to anyone who claimed to be God Almighty. Jesus' declaration that he was a Messiah, merely referred to his earthly desire to ascend to the throne of David--an act of sedition against Rome surely, but not one of blasphemy." http://infidels.org/library/modern/james_still/jesus_trial.html

Jesus certainly does claim to be the SON OF GOD. This position is argued in various ways in the New Testament. Matthew chapter 1 and Luke chapter 1 both present birth narratives in which Jesus is the Son of the Most High/God via Mary's virgin birth, after she was overshadowed by the Holy Spirit. While Mark begins his gospel at Jesus' baptism and does not include a birth narrative, Mark 1:1 speaks of the gospel of Jesus Christ, the son of God. The Gospel of John actually traces Jesus' existence to the LOGOS that became flesh and dwelt among us. That LOGOS, according to John 1:1, was WITH GOD in the beginning and WAS GOD. Matthew 2:15 cites Hosea 11:1 (KJV): "Out of Egypt I have called my son." Even though Hosea's prophecy originally applied to Israel, Matthew extends it to apply to Jesus after his infancy flight to Egypt to escape Herod. At Jesus' baptism, Matthew 3:17, Mark 1:11, and Luke 3:22 report God stating (in the BAT QOL): "This is My beloved son in whom I am well pleased" (KJV). John 1:34 (KJV) has John the Baptist testify: "I have seen and bore witness that this is the Son of God." Immediately following his baptism, Matthew 4:3-6 and Luke 4:3-9 present Jesus' forty days of fasting and temptation in the wilderness with Satan saying, "If you are the Son of God . . ." Matthew 8:29, Mark 5:7, and Luke

8:28 have the Gadarene/Gerasene demoniac/s (and Mark 3:11 and Luke 4:41 have other demon possessed) proclaim that Jesus is "Son of God." John 1:49 (KJV) quotes Nathanael as saying "Rabbi, thou art the Son of God." Matthew 14:33 records Jesus' disciples concluding, after the calming of the sea, "Truly, you are the Son of God." Matthew 16:16 supplies Simon Peter's Great Confession: "You are the Christ, the Son of the Living God." In one of the most famous New Testament verses of all, John 3:16 (KJV) states: "For God so loved the world that He gave His only begotten son . . ." and John 3:18 (KJV) stipulates that to be saved one must believe "on the name of the only begotten Son of God." John 5:25, 9:35, 10:36, and 11:4 have Jesus stating that he is the Son of God. In John 11:27 (KJV), Martha, the sister of Lazarus whom Jesus had raised from the dead, confesses "Yes Lord, I have believed that you are the Christ, the Son of God." Matthew 17:5, Mark 9:7, Luke 9:35, and II Peter 1:17 (KJV) report God, at the Transfiguration, stating (in the BAT QOL): "This is My beloved/chosen son in whom I am well pleased; hear ye him." When High Priest Caiaphas questioned Jesus in an attempt to condemn him, Matthew 26:63-64 and Luke 22:70 (KJV) provide the exchange: "'Tell us whether thou art the Christ, the Son of God.' Jesus replied: 'Thou sayest.'" John 19:7 has the Jewish chief priests demanding that Pilate crucify him because "he made himself the Son of God." While Jesus hung on the cross, mockers, according to Matthew 27:40-43, derided Jesus, saying, "He said, "I am the Son of God." Mark 15:39 tells us that the centurion who witnessed Jesus' death on the cross exclaimed, "Truly, this man was the Son of God." In John 20:31 (KJV), the gospel writer states that he has written his words "that you may believe that Jesus is the Christ, the Son of God." In Acts 8:37, the Ethiopian Eunuch offers up the good confession—"I believe that Jesus Christ is the Son of God"—prior to

Philip baptizing him. In Acts 9:20, the Apostle Paul, after his Road to Damascus experience, begins proclaiming that Jesus is the Son of God. An example of Paul's preaching this creed is found in Acts 13:33 (KJV), citing the second Psalm: "Thou art My Son; this day have I begotten thee." If Luke's account of Paul's belief is insufficient, Paul's own writings (Romans 1:3-9, 5:10, and 8:3 and 29-32, I Corinthians 1:9, II Corinthians 1:19, Galatians 1:16, 2:20, and 4:4-6, Ephesians 4:13, and I Thessalonians 1:10) corroborate the fact. Hebrews 1:5 and 5:5 cite the same Psalm 2 that Acts 13:33 had quoted Paul preaching: "Thou art My Son; this day have I begotten thee." Hebrews 4:14, 6:6, 7:3, and 10:29 reiterate the claim, as do I John 1:3-7, 3:8 and 23, 4:9-15, 5:1-20, II John 3, and Revelation 2:18.

This is the claim made not only by Jesus, but also by many others: that JESUS IS THE CHRIST, THE SON OF GOD. The question is: Is making such a claim "Blasphemy"? Not even James Still, who writes a blog hostile to Christianity, believes that. Even if Jesus were the biological son of Mary and Joseph, Jesus points out from Scripture that there would be nothing wrong with a human claiming to be the Son of God. Jesus is quoted in John 10:33-36 as clearly implying that the term "sons of the Most High" (from Psalm 82:6—a passage I discussed in my book *Angels and demons: The personification of communication* (Chapter 13: Who Are the "Sons of God" in Genesis?) refers to "human judges." Human judges are even called "gods/ELOHIM" in both Psalm 82:6 and Exodus 22:28. Jesus was making the point that it was not blasphemous for him to be called either "god" or "son of God," if even human judges could be called "gods" and "sons of the Most High." In that same book and chapter, I was pointing out that the "Sons of God" in Genesis 6, often mistaken as a reference to angels, is actually a reference to humans. With these multiple biblical references to humans as "sons of God," there is nothing blasphemous in Jesus calling himself "Son of God," even if Jesus were the biological son of Mary and Joseph. Jesus is not guilty of blasphemy.

Is making such a claim a "sin"? Only if it is a lie. Among the Ten Commandments is the prohibition against "bearing false witness." Essentially, if Jesus, his disciples, the BAT QOL, John the Baptist, the evangelists, Paul, and the authors of Hebrews, I and II John, II Peter, and Revelation were all bearing false witness, they would ALL have been sinning. The logic of Christianity says that is not the case. These multiple witnesses (which include God, Himself, in the BAT QOL) assert that Jesus is the Christ, the Son of the Living God.

VIOLATING THE SABBATH

Another commandment from the Decalogue is the Fourth Commandment (Exodus 20:8-11):

> [8] Remember the sabbath day, to keep it holy. [9] Six days shalt thou labour, and do all thy work: [10] But the seventh day is the sabbath of the LORD thy God: in it thou shalt not do any work, thou, nor thy son, nor thy daughter, thy manservant, nor thy maidservant, nor thy cattle, nor thy stranger that is within thy gates: [11] For in six days the LORD made heaven and earth, the sea, and all that in them is, and rested the seventh day: wherefore the LORD blessed the sabbath day, and hallowed it. (KJV)

What, then, constitutes "working" on the Sabbath? During the Exodus, the Israelites were commanded to harvest an extra portion of MANNA on Friday, so that they would not be harvesting on the Sabbath. Nehemiah 13:15 (KJV) states:

In those days saw I in Judah [some] treading wine presses on the sabbath, and bringing in sheaves, and lading asses; as also wine, grapes, and figs, and all [manner of] burdens, which they brought into Jerusalem on the sabbath day: and I testified [against them] in the day wherein they sold victuals.

It seems, by these examples, that "harvesting" and "selling" are considered work that violates the Sabbath. Technically, Jesus' disciples are accused of "harvesting" on the Sabbath, but not Jesus. Mark 2:23 (KJV) reports:

> [23] And it came to pass, that he went through the corn fields on the sabbath day; and his disciples began, as they went, to pluck the ears of corn. [24] And the Pharisees said unto him, Behold, why do they on the sabbath day that which is not lawful? [25] And he said unto them, Have ye never read what David did, when he had need, and was an hungered, he, and they that were with him? [26] How he went into the house of God in the days of Abiathar the high priest, and did eat the shewbread, which is not lawful to eat but for the priests, and gave also to them which were with him? [27] And he said unto them, The sabbath was made for man, and not man for the sabbath: [28] Therefore the Son of man is Lord also of the sabbath.

Matthew's version of this account is found in Matthew 12:1-8. Luke's version of this account is found in Luke 6:1-5. Jesus does not PERSONALLY harvest on the Sabbath, but neither does he condemn his disciples for doing so. His argumentation is presented in the Mark account. Nowhere do we find an Old Testament situation in which "healing" or "saving" an individual is forbidden on the Sabbath. Yet, the gospels present narratives in which Jesus heals on the Sabbath (and even tells one of his healed persons to "take up his bed and walk" on the Sabbath). Jesus argues in Luke 6:9 (KJV): "Is it lawful on the Sabbath to do good, or to do harm? To save a life, or to destroy it?" Luke 14:5 (KJV) presents Jesus as arguing: "Which of you shall have an ass or an ox fallen into a pit, and will not straightway pull him out on the sabbath day?" Matthew 12:11 substitutes a "sheep" for the animals who fell into a pit. Luke 13:15 (NIV) presents Jesus as continuing the analogy: "Doesn't each of you on the Sabbath untie your ox or donkey from the stall and lead it out to give it water?"

DISRESPECT FOR THE HIGH PRIEST

Did Jesus sin by disrespecting the High Priest? You be the judge. John 18:19-23 (NIV) gives the account:

> The high priest then questioned Jesus about his disciples and his teaching. [20] Jesus answered him, "I have spoken openly to the world. I have always taught in synagogues and in the temple, where all Jews come together. I have said nothing in secret. [21] Why do you ask me? Ask those who have heard me what I said to them; they know what I said." [22] When he had said these things, one of the officers standing by struck Jesus with his hand, saying, "Is that how you answer the high priest?" [23] Jesus answered him, "If what I said is wrong, bear witness about the wrong; but if what I said is right, why do you strike me?"

Beyond the fact that this exchange did not suggest any disrespect, Caiaphas was not even a legitimate High Priest. I point out on page 27 of my book *Revelation: The Human Drama*:

It was common knowledge among Jewish leaders that the High Priestly family was indebted to Herod's family for its prestige and power. Antipas' father, Herod the Great, had deposed the then-current (Hasmonean) High Priestly family in the years preceding Jesus' birth. In its place Herod (the Great) had installed a High Priest from among the Jews of the Babylonian Diaspora (those Jews who had been "carried away" into Babylon in the sixth century B.C. and who had not yet returned to Palestine). It is possible that the term "Babylon" in Revelation and I Peter is a code word for this High Priestly family and/or Jerusalem, the city controlled by the (Babylonian?) High Priestly family.

THERE IS NO PROOF THAT JESUS COMMITTED ANY SINS. To the contrary, there is the evidence of the Transfiguration that Jesus lived a perfect life. So, did Jesus receive JUSTICE? The best definition of "justice" that mankind, throughout history, has ever been able to formulate is called the LEX TALIONIS (An eye for an eye, a tooth for a tooth, a life for a life). It means that an individual who has injured another may be punished only to the degree s/he has injured. It is found in the Law of Moses (Leviticus 24:19-21, and other places). But it is also found in the ancient Code of Hammurabi, a Babylonian law code carved in stone from about 1750 B.C. It served not as a "requirement" that someone be avenged to the same degree as the injury; rather, it was the maximum "limit" of revenge (or reTALIation—a word stemming from the same root as TALIonis) that could be exacted. This would be the full extent of JUSTICE. Therefore, if Jesus committed no sins, no injuries to anyone, JUSTICE could not allow him to even be KILLED, much less be CRUCIFIED! Indeed, true JUSTICE for a person who committed no sins would be something like the TRANSFIGURATION, which Jesus was offered but did not seize hold of. One might guess that Elijah, Enoch, and (perhaps) Moses were offered this sort of JUSTICE. Of those three, Enoch was the only one to live prior to the Law of Moses, so it is easy to argue that (since he was living under fewer laws) he had an easier pathway to translation than did Moses or Elijah. Elijah, while living under the Law, reached the point in his life at which God took him to heaven in a Fiery Chariot. Hence, Elijah received justice. One would think that, since Moses was the actual Law Giver, he would be well aware of the full ramifications and details of every single law he gave. Before he gave those laws, obviously, there was no "Law of Moses," so the earlier part of Moses' life would have been subject to the same laws that Enoch was subject to. Therefore, Moses might be capable of living a perfect life according to the Law. If the fact that he appears with Elijah on the Mount of Transfiguration suggests that he did live the Law, Moses received justice. But, alongside these three righteous individuals, Jesus as a righteous individual, suffered one of the most degrading and excruciating punishments known to man.

It may surprise you, but my ANSWER to the question "DID JESUS RECEIVE JUSTICE" is YES! Based upon the principle of the LEX TALIONIS, Jesus received "justice," but not justice for any sin he personally committed. Crucifixion is a horrible punishment, reserved for only the WORST CRIMINALS in the Roman Empire. I return to the very first chapter in this book (pages 1 & 2): I recall the point at which my wife and I were shown the evidence contained in the Shroud of Turin:

> Using a variety of scientific methods, we were able to observe visible signs of a face with thorn wounds around the head, of hands and feet that had been pierced by nails, of a back that had been scourged by whips, of a stab wound in the side--a victim of crucifixion identical to the biblical description of Jesus' crucifixion.

Part of the awe-inspiring experience of viewing the Shroud of Turin was just gaining a glimpse into the physical signs of what a crucifixion victim experienced. Before Jesus was nailed to the cross, to experience the excruciating pain of having large iron nails hammered through the flesh in each of his wrists and through both of his feet securely into the wood of the cross . . . Before he—nailed to the cross—was, hanging by only these nail points, lifted skyward, and dropped joltingly upon his cross into the hole in the ground at the base of the cross . . . Before he was degraded, humiliated, and exposed naked on the cross (a factor that we don't even share among Christians, due to the embarrassment caused by even thinking of the picture) . . . Before he thus hung, suspended above the Earth, for hours, while his body experienced dehydration, pain, and the slow process of dying . . . Before he was forced to carry the agency of his crucifixion—a wooden cross large and heavy enough to hold the full weight of a man—through the streets of Jerusalem and uphill, all the way to Golgotha . . . Before he was mocked, dressed in purple, slapped repeatedly, and given a crown, comprised of nail-like thorns, which was jammed painfully into the flesh of his head . . . Before he was scourged to the limit with flesh-tearing whips and scourges until the open wounds on his back bled profusely . . . He had to witness one of his closest friends and disciples curse and deny any connection with him. Now, that is probably JUSTICE . . . .Justice for a bin Laden who masterminded the mass murder of thousands on 9-11. Justice for a Hitler who ordered the genocide of six million Jews. Justice for a Jeffrey Dahmer, whose atrocities I recounted in Chapter 5. None of those three were forced to go through a punishing death anywhere near as severe as Jesus' crucifixion. They received nothing remotely near what would be allowable under the LEX TALIONIS.

So, we can each think retrospectively: What sins have I committed? Have I even unintentionally committed murder? Have I committed manslaughter by driving under the influence of alcohol? Have I performed, recommended, or decided to have an abortion? Have I had to make a decision to remove life support for a family member, and experienced conscientious stress over the decision? Have I had to issue a command to send men or women into combat in which they lost their lives, and experienced conscientious stress over the decision? Have I cheated on my husband or wife? Have I practiced homosexuality? Have I embezzled money or committed fraud? Have I dishonored my father or mother? Have I taken the Lord's Name in vain? Have I coveted another person's wife or husband, house, money, etc.? Thinking of the LEX TALIONIS, what should we think the fair maximum penalty could possibly be? Could it be any worse than CRUCIFIXION? What kind of sin or crime could one possibly commit that would suggest a fair maximum penalty greater than Crucifixion? I cannot think of one. If that is so, Jesus' Crucifixion was JUSTICE for any sin known to mankind. Jesus did receive justice. He received justice, not for his own actions, but for the actions of any human that has ever lived. He paid the price. The CRUCIFIXION, then, is Judicial Rhetoric/The Justice Link in the Logic of Christianity.

Chapter 10

Full Circle Logic: The Resurrection

The LOGIC OF THE UNIVERSE IS CIRCULAR. This is not the same as saying that the universe

uses "circular reasoning" (also known as "circular logic"), which is what logicians call a "logical

fallacy." A logical fallacy is an incorrect form of logic. Circular reasoning takes two opposing-

but-incapable-of-being-absolutely-proved assertions, negates one, and then proves the one by

citing the negative of the other. For example, the argument that "atheism is correct because there

is no god" is circular reasoning, a logical fallacy. The argument that "women are smarter than

men because men are dumber" is circular reasoning. The argument that "broccoli tastes better

than peas because peas taste worse" is circular reasoning.

When I suggest that the logic of the universe is circular, I mean that everything in the operation of

the universe employs circularity/cycles.   I offer empirical evidence: Virtually everything that operates in the physical world is circular. I point out in my book *Hidden Mickeyisms: The Implicit Rhetoric of Disney Films* (Chapter 1: "Cosmic Circles and Mickey Mouse"):

> We understand a "circle round the sun" [from Epcot's fireworks theme song] to refer to a year, 365 days. . . . Not only does the *earth* circle the sun, but *other planets* do, as well. The "thousand circles" may refer to a millennium, but each millennium is exponentially compounded by the thousand circles of other planets. How many millennia has the earth existed? And isn't every decade, century, and millennium also a circle of sorts? The number of circles in the universe is again exponentially compounded. For that matter, while the earth is circling the sun once, it is also rotating in a circle on its axis 365 times. These are 365 additional circles to factor in. And once, every 28 days, the earth's relationship to its moon creates another circle—a month . . . Remember also that the sun is only one of billions of stars, all of which have their own circling planets, and those planets, their moons. . . . Don't forget that these stars all seem to be circling within their own galaxies. The Milky Way is only one circular galaxy, with countless circles occurring within. . . . Now, consider the atom with its nucleus, and circling protons and neutrons, and . . . every planet, moon, star, asteroid, and meteor is comprised of countless atoms. . . . Each circle has a beginning, middle, and end. And, once each circle completes one entelechy (one circle), it begins a new entelechy (a new circle). . . . Of course, Aristotle is not content to consider . . . only astrophysical circles. He is primarily interested in geophysical and biological entelechies. The circle of a drop of rain falling from the sky, running from a stream of water into a creek, then into a river, then into the sea, after which it evaporates into the atmosphere and helps form a cloud, until it becomes too heavy and eventually condenses and becomes a drop of rain again is an entelechy, a circle. A kernel of corn is planted in the earth. It puts forth roots, then a blade, which becomes a stalk. The stalk develops leaves,

tassels, and ears—composed of husks, silks, and cobs. The cobs develop rows and rows of kernels. Once these kernels of corn have matured, have fully ripened, these kernels are ready to begin new entelechies, new circles. . . . There is the biological "Circle of Life," as Disney's *Lion King* names it. That circle includes not only the circle of biological reproduction and maturation of every single animal, followed by another reproduction and maturation, etc. It also includes the circle of the food chain, the circular nature of the respiratory, circulatory, and digestive systems of each biological organism, and so on.

On the front cover of my book *Revelation: The Human Drama* is the image of a circular snake (OUROBOROS) with its tail being swallowed by its head, signifying that a circle starts at the head and proceeds to end at the tail, which, in turn begins again at the head. In the center of this circular snake is an image of Eve picking the forbidden fruit. The point of the image is that the entire human drama is a circle. When Revelation refers to the "Alpha and Omega, the First and the Last, the Beginning and the End," it is referring to the CIRCULARITY OF THE HISTORY OF MANKIND, even the circularity of the history of the universe (from creation to destruction to new creation). Logically, in terms of the circle of the history of mankind, Genesis begins with Adam and Eve, living an immortal (or, at least, a non-dying) life. Their free-will is tested with the first hortatory negative—Thou shalt not eat of the Tree of Knowledge of Good and Evil—combined with the threat of "Death" should they violate this rule. They, with their free will, respond by eating and the dying process begins. Immediately, a new (inferior) circle begins. This INFERIOR

CIRCLE is the biological, birth-maturation-reproduction (followed by death) circle—the same biological circle that is found in all biological forms. We notice that the biological circle has begun, according to Genesis, in the respect that the reproductive impulse is present in Adam and Eve immediately following the eating of the forbidden fruit—for the first time, they notice their own nakedness. To this day, the biological circle for humans is invoked for consolation purposes at funerals: "S/he lives on through his/her children!" But, this biological circle is a substitute for what was originally presented as the beginning of an ETERNAL LIFE CIRCLE. The immortal beings (Adam and Eve) became mortal (through a <u>lapse of faith</u>). The full-circle logic of the eternal life circle would be the reclaiming of immortality through the <u>exercise of absolute faith</u> (the single failure to exercise of which Adam and Eve were guilty). Hence, Revelation presents its Conquerors as those individuals who had so much faith in Jesus that they were willing to be martyred. Just as Adam had lost faith in God's word to him and received Death in the bargain, these Conquerors were willing to accept Death as a martyr as the ultimate proof that they believed in God and Jesus and received Eternal Life in the bargain.

The COSMIC CIRCLE OF THE LOGIC OF ETERNAL LIFE begins with the very first man, Adam. He is created in the image of God. In other words, he possesses free will, communicates using symbols/words that he himself creates, is capable of making not only his own symbols-words-grammar, but also his own tools and his own tools for making other tools, etc. He is also in the image of God in the sense that he is IMMORTAL. Then, in his exercise of free will, he CHOOSES to doubt God. Upon choosing to eat that which God had warned him not to eat, he becomes mortal, and within his inferior circle (biological reproductive circle), he begins to procreate as a FALLEN MAN. His offspring, being the product of his inferior biological reproductive circle, is born into the same FALLEN STATE as Adam and Eve (the biological product of the Original Sin). A very few individuals (Enoch, Elijah, and possibly Moses) prove that, by following God's explicit commands verbatim throughout their lives, that it is possible—through living perfect lives—to regain immortality (at least, for themselves) through translation (Enoch) or fiery chariots (Elijah), etc. Then, Jesus as a human being accomplishes the same feat as Elijah and is rewarded with TRANSFIGURATION. Unlike Elijah who had achieved immortality on his own, Jesus gives back his own personal prize. He accepts the penalty of death by crucifixion to satisfy the judgments and sentences that were pending for all mankind that had not, like Elijah, earned eternal life, for themselves. So, with the RESURRECTION OF JESUS, we come FULL CIRCLE—bringing mankind (THE SEED OF ADAM) back to IMMORTALITY. The tail of the snake OUROBOROS has, once again, reached its head. Adam was immortal, at first, and now, Adam and his seed have had the immortality restored. The Alpha is the same as the Omega. The First is the same as the Last. The Beginning is the same as the End.

[As an aside, I now return full circle to Chapter 1: "The Shroud, the Pope, and the Faith Continuum." The Shroud of Turin, whether it is ACTUALLY the burial shroud of Jesus, at the very least, REPRESENTS the burial shroud of Jesus. And, as has been proposed by some of the archaeological scholars who have examined it, may show signs of a photographic light image on the shroud (which would be the equivalent of film). The light that may have produced this photographic effect could have been produced by a resurrecting Jesus. Once again, whether this postulation is considered 99% credible or only .00001% credible, even the hint of faith in the possibility that it is true is still "faith."]

I will leave to others the responsibility of marshalling the evidence that Jesus' resurrection occurred. Many have done excellent work, in that respect. But since this is a book on the "Logic of Christianity," I will be content with presenting the logic of the resurrection. The Toulminian logic looks like this:

WARRANT: The logic of the universe is circular, not linear.

DATA: If mankind began in an immortal state, and then was reduced forever to mortality, that would be linear movement, not circular.

CLAIM: Therefore, the concept of an immortal beginning with a mortal ending is illogical (being linear, not circular).

REBUTTAL: Unless there is no hint in the biblical account that recorded the First Man's early immortal state and fall to mortality that there would be a return to the immortal state.

BACKING: But, there is a hint of a future return to immortality: Genesis 3:15 (KJV), just nine verses after the account of the eating of the Forbidden Fruit, hints at the circular logic: "And I will put enmity between thee and the woman, and between thy seed and her seed; it shall bruise thy head, and thou shalt bruise his heel." Is Genesis 3:15 suggesting that the inferior act of [the Serpent] taking away man's immortality will be supplanted by the superior act of bruising the Serpent's head [understand: killing the killer of mankind?] by one of woman's seed.

QUALIFIER: "Definitely"-- Therefore, the concept of an immortal beginning with a mortal ending is DEFINITELY illogical.

While the earliest foreshadowing of the route this ETERNAL LIFE CIRCLE will take is found in the words of Genesis 3:15, Genesis 5:22-24 records the account of Enoch who "was not for God took him"—an indication that the writer of Genesis believed in immortality, at least, for some. There is the further hint in Deuteronomy 34 that the mysterious disappearance of Moses' corpse at the end of his life was pregnant with possibilities of immortality. Job 19:25-26 (KJV) indicates that resurrection was expected by non-Israelites, since Job was a descendent of Esau, not Jacob (Israel): "For I know that my redeemer liveth, and that he shall stand at the latter day upon the earth. And though after my skin worms destroy this body, yet in my flesh shall I see God." Abraham appears to believe that God will resurrect Isaac after he sacrifices him. He tells his servants in Genesis 22:5 (KJV): "Abide ye here with the ass; and I and the lad will go yonder and worship and come again to you." Hebrews 11:18-19 (KJV) interprets this hint: "Of whom it was said that in Isaac shall thy seed be called: Accounting that God was able to raise him up, even from the dead; from whence also he received him . . ." Three Old Testament individuals were actually resurrected (albeit, to mortal bodies, not immortal bodies, even as, in the New Testament, Lazarus, the daughter of Jairus, and the son of the widow of Nain were raised by Jesus, and Peter and Paul each raised individuals—to mortal bodies). Daniel 12:2 (KJV), however, makes the explicit promise of a future resurrection to immortality: "And many of them that sleep in the dust of the earth shall awake, some to everlasting life, and some to shame and everlasting contempt."

Jesus' resurrection accomplishes the first such resurrection to immortality and, thus, ushers in FULL CIRCLE LOGIC.

Chapter 11

Any Proofs that the Resurrection Never Happened?

The first historical attempt to deny that Jesus arose from the dead is described in Matthew 28:11-15. Matthew's audience (living decades after the crucifixion) is, apparently, still very much aware of an explanation offered among Jews for the disappearance of Jesus' body: The Roman Guards who were securing the tomb holding Jesus' body, according to the explanation, all fell asleep during their watch. Jesus' disciples, of course, sensing that this likelihood would "probably" occur (wink and nod—I'm mocking, here), had the cunning, alertness, and presence of mind to immediately capitalize on the Guards' temporary lapse to sneak in quietly, roll the stone away, and steal Jesus' body, thus violating the Commandment against working on the Sabbath at the same time they were violating Roman law, since the purported theft involved the illegal breaking of the seal of the Roman procurator, Pontius Pilate. How the Guards who were soundly asleep could possibly have known that a "theft" of the body had occurred is not explained. If the Guards were truly asleep during this purported theft, they would not know at all what had happened to the body. If one of them had awakened during the process (and, hence, noticed the theft occurring), he would have, most certainly, alerted his fellow guards and disrupted the theft. Surely, at least one of the thieves would have been captured or some physical evidence of a dead body being moved would have been discovered. Furthermore, if a theft of a dead body that had been sealed in a tomb by Pilate were accomplished, where would the disciples hide this dead body that, by now, had begun to stink? Why is it that, even decades after the purported theft (in Matthew's account), no physical evidence of the stolen body of Jesus had ever been located? The only "proof" offered in this scenario is the "EYE-WITNESS TESTIMONY" of Guards WHO CLAIM TO HAVE BEEN "ASLEEP" WHEN IT HAPPENED.

Abdullah Kareem, in his web post, "The Resurrection Hoax" (http://answering-christianity.com/abdullah_smith/the_resurrection_hoax.htm) argues that the resurrection of Jesus is a hoax because Mark, the earliest gospel, "never contained the story." Mr. Kareem's use of the term "never" is quite clearly erroneous. (If Kareem were a biblical author, the anti-Christian forces would surely swoop down to demonstrate that he can have no claim to inerrancy!) Some early manuscripts of Mark contain Mark 16:9-20, which recounts resurrection appearances to Mary Magdalene, the Eleven apostles, and two men walking in the country. So, one cannot say that Mark "never" contained the story. Kareem's claim might be more correctly phrased: "The earliest manuscripts of the Gospel of Mark do not contain the accounts of resurrection appearances to Mary Magdalene, the Eleven apostles, and two men walking in the country." That much is true, but that does not mean that Mark did not contain the resurrection story. In a passage that is not disputed by textual critics, Mark 16:1-8 contains the early Easter morning story of Mary Magdalene and two others coming to anoint Jesus' body. They found the stone rolled away from the mouth of the tomb, and upon entering, they saw a person robed in white who said to them, "Be not afraid. You are looking for Jesus the Nazarene, who was crucified. He is risen; He is not here; see the place where they laid him." Mr. Kareem's argument, therefore, is again erroneous. Even without Mark 16:9-20, Mark still contains the resurrection story. Mr. Kareem continues with innuendo and slanted arguments, none of which are particularly compelling, and then closes with this challenge: "We challenge Christians to prove his resurrection."

The problem with Mr. Kareem's challenge is that it presumes that the burden of proof rests upon Christians. Who says it does? Who gets to decide which "presumptions" should take precedence? In American jurisprudence, we constitutionally grant a "presumption of innocence" to anyone who is accused of a crime. We say that s/he is presumed innocent, until proven guilty. But, who could prove that this presumption is the best presumption? Why not presume that anyone who is accused is guilty, until proven innocent? The answer is that "cultures" decide which presumptions the cultures will accept. In my book, *ArguMentor* (p. 69), I discuss "those 'starting points' of Perelman's argumentation—those facts, truths, and presumptions—that each specific culture *unconsciously* admits." Put differently, there are no "facts," unless the culture in which one states the fact admits that it is a fact. Especially, in the postmodern era, there are no "truths," unless the culture in which one states the truth admits that it is a truth. And, we cannot "presume" anything unless the culture in which we expect the "presumption" to hold sway admits that it is the acceptable presumption. Foss, Foss, and Trapp, in their acclaimed work *Contemporary Perspectives on Rhetoric* (p. 89) note:

> [T]he audience's adherence to presumptions falls short of being maximum; thus, presumptions, unlike facts and truths, can be reinforced by argumentation. Speakers engage in preliminary argumentation to establish certain presumptions or to reinforce the presumptions in the minds of the audience. . . . [P]resumptions can be violated, whereas facts and truths cannot.

Perelman states on pages 24-25 of the *Realm of Rhetoric* that presumption "imposes the burden of proof upon the person who wants to oppose its application." So, I disagree with Abdullah Kareem's assessment of the presumptions when it comes to the resurrection of Jesus. My position is that, given the 2000-year-long general acceptance in western culture of the resurrection, the burden of proof is on Mr. Kareem to prove that it did NOT happen. And, I challenge anyone to prove that the resurrection did not happen. How would someone even begin to go about proving such a thing? For that matter, how would someone prove that God did NOT create the universe? How would someone prove that the Bible is NOT inspired of God? These are some of my presumptions:

- The resurrection did occur.

- God did create the universe.

- The Bible is inspired of God.

Furthermore, they are presumptions held by a massive Christian Culture. My presumption is that these premises are "true, until proven false." I will stipulate that NOT ALL who study the Scriptures admit these presumptions. There was a major paradigm shift in biblical studies around the turn of the 20th Century—probably, the result of (a now discredited) modernist philosophy and the application of Occam's Razor. In his book *Between Faith and Criticism*, Mark A. Noll writes of two biblical studies cultures operating under opposing presumptions (p.7):

> The story of these clashing communities is, however, really two stories. Of most interest to outsiders is the record of traditional Bible-believers first competing in the intellectual marketplace as full partners in the academic discussion of Scripture (roughly 1880 to 1900); then retreating from that world to the fortress of faith (roughly 1900 to 1935); then slowly realizing the values of some participation in that wider world (1935 to 1950), finding the strategies to put themselves back in the professional picture once again (1940 to 1975), and finally confronting new spiritual and intellectual dilemmas because of success in those ventures (1960 to the present). This part of the story is largely an account of . . . conflicting ASSUMPTIONS about the Bible (emphasis mine).

On page 45, Noll observes that, after 1900, "a new paradigm emerges for the practice of normal science (The Bible, however sublime, is a human book to be investigated with the standard ASSUMPTIONS that one brings to the discussion of all products of human culture [emphasis mine])." Replace the term "assumptions" in the quotations I have cited above (and placed in all caps) with the term "presumptions" and you will have a better grasp of the "logical" situation I am describing. The difference is that when the new paradigm emerged, the term "assumption" for the advocates of considering the Bible to be a human book became much more of a "premise" or a "creed" than an "assumption" or "presumption." In other words, advocates of considering the Bible to be a human book leave no room for the possibility of being proven wrong. For them, the description of the Bible is not "human until proven divine" in a way analogous to our legal formula: "innocent until proven guilty." They simply allow no room for the possibility of their assumption being wrong. There is no way they would grant the Bible any divine nature. It is as if their "assumption" takes on the full weight of "truth." It is, therefore, with much more humility that I advance the "presumption" formula concerning the Bible that it is "divinely inspired until proven human;" that it is "true until proven false." This more humble "presumption" of mine is akin to the postmodern view expressed in 1974 by University of Chicago Professor Wayne C. Booth in *Modern Dogma and the Rhetoric of Assent*: "It is reasonable to grant (one ought to grant) some degree of credence to whatever qualified men and women agree on, unless one has specific and stronger reasons to disbelieve" (101).

"Granting some degree of credence" is another formula for defining the term "faith." In Chapter 1: The Shroud, the Pope, and the Faith Continuum, I remarked: "Even miniscule faith in a tiny possibility is still faith." I offered extreme examples:

> Faith is a continuum. It runs all the way from the tiniest, faintest possibility that something is true (such as the faint possibility that I was within 15 to 20 feet of the actual DNA of Jesus [at the Shroud of Turin]) to the almost certain probability that something is true (such as the almost certain fact that I was within 15 to 20 feet of Pope Francis [in St. Peter's Square of the Vatican]).

I cited Aristotle to the following effect:

> Faith . . . must admit at least two possibilities. In his book, *On Rhetoric*, Aristotle teaches how rhetorical logic works. In rhetoric (as opposed to dialectic), the aim is not to provide absolute truth, but only possible or probable truth. It applies only to matters of which we cannot be certain. Nevertheless, although certainty is impossible, we can logically conclude that something is "probably" or "possibly" true. Aristotle says that the goal of this type of logic is to achieve "faith."

With this chapter, I am further positing that "faith" is the accepting of presumptions. I stated that some of my presumptions include the following:

- The resurrection did occur.

- God did create the universe.

- The Bible is inspired of God.

Furthermore, I pointed out, they are presumptions held by a massive Christian Culture. My presumption is that these premises are "true, until proven false." That, for me, is the essence of effective Christian faith. Although I argued that even atheists possess a small degree of faith in God, I would not consider such miniscule faith to be "effective Christian faith." Effective Christian faith begins at the point one chooses to join the culture that accepts presumptions such as those identified above. Accepting these presumptions does not mean that one must relegate his or her brain and cognitive powers to the closet. It means simply that Christians give God, Jesus, the Bible, the Resurrection, etc. the benefit of the doubt. We will believe that these presumptions are "true until proven false."

Simply shifting the burden of proof from the believers to the unbelievers produces stunning results. If unbelievers must prove that the resurrection did not occur, I believe they would need some powerful evidence: the physical remains of Jesus' body, uncontested confessions from some of his close followers that a hoax had been perpetrated, etc. If unbelievers must prove that there is no God or that He did not create the universe, they would need to produce evidence that it is impossible to produce. If unbelievers must prove that the Bible is false, they must first determine every possible meaning of every Greek, Hebrew, and Aramaic word in the Scriptures. Then, they must consider every conceivable grammatical combination in which those words may be found. Next, they must consider every possible trope, every figure of speech, as a means of determining the multitudinous possible interpretations of every verse of scripture. And, they must disprove not just one or two interpretations that they might prefer to debunk, in a "straw man" logical fallacy approach. They must disprove every single interpretation that is remotely possible—that has been previously advanced or that will be advanced at any point in the future.

In my academic career, I frequently pursue the interpretive "possibilities" of biblical texts, and my pursuits are often guided by the debunking activities of some of my fellow scholars who have chosen to follow unbelieving presumptions. If unbelieving scholars attempt to debunk a "young earth" interpretation of Genesis, I pursue the possibilities in the Hebrew text to see if any evidence of an "older earth" interpretation is possible. If unbelieving scholars attempt to assert evolutionary biological theories, I investigate the language used in Genesis. My goal is not to cave on creationist theologies, but to investigate the range of possibilities. What if the interpretations accepted by generations of Christians are incorrect—as, for example, many Christians still mistakenly identify "Lucifer" in Isaiah with "Satan"? I was raised in a non-denominational Christian movement that pledged no allegiance to man-made creeds. I am not committed to defending the various Christian creeds developed over the last two millennia. I do not presume them to be inspired. I do, on the other hand, presume that the Bible is inspired, and in the next few chapters, I will offer some of the new perspectives I have pursued in investigating some of the texts unbelieving scholars have attacked. My faith remains unscathed.

Chapter 12

In God's Own Handwriting

According to the Bible, God, PERSONALLY, only wrote two messages to mankind: one message in ARAMAIC and one message in HEBREW. The message in Aramaic was the "Handwriting on the Wall" incident recorded in the book Daniel (5:25): "MN' MN' TKL PRS PRS." So far as we know, the handwriting of God, in this instance, was preserved only long enough for Daniel to decipher it and interpret its meaning for the Babylonian king Belshazzar. It had to do with God's warning of the impending break-up of the Babylonian Empire. (God has had an inclination toward breaking up mighty human institutions of power, over the millennia: the Tower of Babel; the Greek and Roman Empires; perhaps even, the Catholic Church in the Reformation? Nazi Germany? the Soviet Union? Are the American political parties next?) This chapter is not primarily concerned with the Daniel handwriting.

Instead, this chapter focuses on the PREMIER HANDWRITTEN MESSAGE FROM GOD: THE

TEN COMMANDMENTS. We begin the discussion of the defensibility of the presumption that

the Bible is true and divine until proven false with the single piece of divine communication that

was so revered that it was carried before the people of Israel for centuries in its own protective

container, the Ark of the Covenant, which was itself most highly revered: "And thou shalt put into

the ark the testimony which I shall give thee" (Exodus 25:16 [KJV]).

> So I made the ark out of acacia wood and chiseled out two stone tablets like the
> first ones, and I went up to the mountain with the two tablets in my hands. The Lord
> wrote on these tablets what He had written before, the Ten Commandments He had
> proclaimed to you on the mountain, out of the fire, on the day of the assembly. And
> The Lord gave them to me. Then I came back down the mountain and put the tablets
> in the ark I had made, as The Lord commanded me, and they are there now.
> Deuteronomy 10:3-5 (NIV)

> ...which had the golden altar of incense and the gold-covered ark of the covenant.
> This ark contained the gold jar of manna, Aaron's staff that had budded, and the
> stone tablets of the covenant. Hebrews 9:4 (NIV)

Jewish scribes, from the time of the New Testament and before, prioritized the importance of the

messages they had received from God. They distinguished, even in their Bible, which they called

the TaNaCH (an alliteration), between the T (for TORAH—translated "Law"—the first five

books), the N (for NEVI'IM—translated "Prophets"), and the CH (for CHETUVIM—translated

"Writings" or "Hagiographa"—which included Psalms, Proverbs, Job, Song of Solomon, Ruth,

Lamentations, Ecclesiastes, Esther, Daniel, Ezra, Nehemiah, and First and Second Chronicles). The CHETUVIM were not considered as authoritative as the Law and the Prophets. According to the statistics found in Nestle-Aland's Greek New Testament, even the New Testament <u>fails to cite any text or make literary allusion whatsoever</u> pointing to such Old Testament books as Ruth, Ezra, Song of Solomon, or Ecclesiastes. Other CHETUVIM, such as First and Second Chronicles, Nehemiah, Esther, and Lamentations each <u>receive only one slight (and fairly unimportant) literary allusion</u> apiece in the New Testament. On the other hand, there are numerous citations and allusions in the New Testament to Psalms, Proverbs, Job, and Daniel, among the CHETUVIM, as well as numerous citations and allusions to ALL OF THE LAW AND THE PROPHETS. Therefore, other than the CHETUVIM books—Psalms, Proverbs, Job, and Daniel—some Christians might not spend a great deal of effort defending the inspiration and infallibility of the CHETUVIM. I would not personally excommunicate someone who believes s/he may have found a problem in one of these books (for example, a narrative account in Chronicles that differs with one in Samuel or Kings). It is not 100% necessary that such a specific problem should negatively impact that person's faith in the Bible as the inspired Word of God. There is no incontrovertible argument to be made that Paul had in mind these CHETUVIM texts that are barely alluded to—if even alluded to, at all—in the New Testament, when he stated that "all scripture is given by inspiration of God, and is profitable for doctrine, for reproof, for correction, for instruction in righteousness" (2 Timothy 3:16 [KJV]). Samaritans, Sadducees, Pharisees, and the New Testament all appear to give these CHETUVIM texts less priority.

Although the New Testament cites and alludes to Psalms, Proverbs, Job, and Daniel (among the CHETUVIM) as well as to every book in the Law and the Prophets, it should be pointed out that the Samaritans believed that only the Torah/Law/Pentateuch was inspired (See John 4). If the Sadducees believed that there was any inspiration in the Prophets, they held that the inspiration was inferior to the inspiration of the Torah/Law/Pentateuch (See Acts 23:5-7). The Pharisees, as well as Jesus and the Christians, believed that both the Law and the Prophets were inspired. Furthermore, the Pharisees expanded the "Law" to include the "Oral Law." They claimed that Moses had handed down more laws than were written in the first five books, and that these laws were passed on by oral tradition from rabbi to rabbi (until finally written down in the Talmud). The New Testament rejected this "oral law" tradition (See Matthew 15, Mark 7, and Galatians 1). The Pharisees, however, believed the Law (or legal sections of the Law) to be superior, and even in the Law, they made the distinction between HALAKHAH (the sections of actual laws) and AGGADAH (everything else).

So, to begin at the very beginning of inspired scripture, we start with the actual HALAKHAH from the hand of God: The Ten Commandments, or Decalogue. How could any message of God be attributed a higher priority! Moses first received the Decalogue on Mount Sinai, as God carved out two stone tablets and wrote the Commandments on them with his own hand (Exodus 31:18). But when Moses came down the mountain with the first two tablets, he found the Israelites worshipping idols. In his wrath, Moses smashed the two tablets to the ground (Exodus 32:19). After purging the evil from Israel, God told Moses to cut out two more tablets, like the first two, and God again wrote in his own handwriting on the tablets, in Hebrew, the Decalogue (Exodus 34:1-4). The words of the Decalogue are found in Exodus 20:2-17 (KJV):

"I am the LORD thy God, which have brought thee out of the land of Egypt, out of the house of bondage.

3Thou shalt have no other gods before me.

4Thou shalt not make unto thee any graven image, or any likeness of any thing that is in heaven above, or that is in the earth beneath, or that is in the water under the earth:

5Thou shalt not bow down thyself to them, nor serve them: for I the LORD thy God am a jealous God, visiting the iniquity of the fathers upon the children unto the third and fourth generation of them that hate me;

6And shewing mercy unto thousands of them that love me, and keep my commandments.

7Thou shalt not take the name of the LORD thy God in vain; for the LORD will not hold him guiltless that taketh his name in vain.

8Remember the sabbath day, to keep it holy.

9Six days shalt thou labour, and do all thy work:

10But the seventh day is the sabbath of the LORD thy God: in it thou shalt not do any work, thou, nor thy son, nor thy daughter, thy manservant, nor thy maidservant, nor thy cattle, nor thy stranger that is within thy gates:

11For in six days the LORD made heaven and earth, the sea, and all that in them is, and rested the seventh day: wherefore the LORD blessed the sabbath day, and hallowed it.

12Honour thy father and thy mother: that thy days may be long upon the land which the LORD thy God giveth thee.

13Thou shalt not kill.

14Thou shalt not commit adultery.

15Thou shalt not steal.

16Thou shalt not bear false witness against thy neighbour.

17Thou shalt not covet thy neighbour's house, thou shalt not covet thy neighbour's wife, nor his manservant, nor his maidservant, nor his ox, nor his ass, nor any thing that is thy neighbour's."

The first three commandments (verses 2 through 7) pertain to the argument that God/YHWH is the one true god. I have already argued this truth, earlier, in Chapter 5: The God of Logic vs. Jeffrey Dahmer, and Chapter 6: WHODUNNIT? Responding in the proper manner to the one true God is the individual's FIRST PRIORITY. Commandment Four reminds the individual that the individual's SECOND PRIORITY is to respond to his/her source—his/her father and mother—in the proper manner. Commandments Six, Seven, Eight, Nine, and Ten seem to PRIORITIZE THE MORAL LAWS individuals must live by: First, don't murder. Second, don't have sex with someone who is not one's spouse. Third, don't steal someone else's property. Fourth, don't falsely testify against another human. And, Fifth, avoid even the practice of even desiring something that belongs to another human.

Stuck in between the individual's responsibilities to God and ones parents and the individual's responsibilities to ones fellow human beings is a curious commandment that pertains to the individual's responsibilities to onesself: Remember the Sabbath Day. Jesus argues that the Sabbath Day was made for humans, not vice versa. Rest (one definition of Sabbath) is something individuals are required to do for themselves. God gave laws that humans must obey for their own good! Humans need a day of rest, at least once per week. But, one thing that might be easily overlooked in this Sabbath commandment is the interesting basis upon which God gave humans the Sabbath—THE FACT THAT HE "CREATED" THE WORLD IN JUST SIX DAYS, AND THEN RESTED ON THE SEVENTH. There it is! Right there, in God's own handwriting! God CREATED the world! This is not AGGADAH! This is HALAKHAH! This is the one passage to which everyone gives priority—the Ten Commandments! The handwriting of God! Creation is not a myth. It is not folklore. It is LAW/ HALAKHAH. In the next chapter, I'll explore some of the attacks that have been made on the Creation Account, keeping in mind our presumption: True until proven False!

Chapter 13

Creation is True until Proven False

Two chapters ago, I threw down the gauntlet: **"IF UNBELIEVERS MUST PROVE THAT THE BIBLE IS FALSE, THEY MUST FIRST DETERMINE EVERY POSSIBLE MEANING OF EVERY GREEK, HEBREW, AND ARAMAIC WORD IN THE SCRIPTURES. THEN, THEY MUST CONSIDER EVERY CONCEIVABLE GRAMMATICAL COMBINATION IN WHICH THOSE WORDS MAY BE FOUND. NEXT, THEY MUST CONSIDER EVERY POSSIBLE TROPE, EVERY FIGURE OF SPEECH, AS A MEANS OF DETERMINING THE MULTITUDINOUS POSSIBLE INTERPRETATIONS OF EVERY VERSE OF SCRIPTURE. AND, THEY MUST DISPROVE NOT JUST ONE OR TWO INTERPRETATIONS THAT THEY MIGHT PREFER TO DEBUNK, IN A "STRAW MAN" LOGICAL FALLACY APPROACH. THEY MUST DISPROVE EVERY SINGLE INTERPRETATION THAT IS REMOTELY POSSIBLE—THAT HAS BEEN**

PREVIOUSLY ADVANCED OR THAT WILL BE ADVANCED AT ANY POINT IN THE FUTURE."

So, what elements of the Genesis creation account do unbelievers doubt?

1. They doubt that the universe was created by any "god." (They prefer a non-purposive Big Bang theory, instead.)

2. They doubt that the universe came into existence within the time span indicated by Genesis. (They prefer a much longer time frame than they think Genesis supplies.)

3. They doubt that the order of the elements of the universe coming into existence is correctly indicated in Genesis. (Specifically, they object to the timing of the appearance in Genesis of the Sun, Moon, and Stars.)

4. They doubt that any "god" was active in the progressive expansion of life forms. (They prefer a non-purposive "evolutionary" model instead.)

5. They doubt that man was made "in the image" of any god. (They prefer a behaviorist view of man: that like all other animals, man behaves in predictable, non-creative ways.)

6. They doubt that Adam was a specific distinct creation. (They prefer an evolutionary model of the development of man/*Homo sapiens*: from Neanderthal or Heidelberg man.)

My book *Disneology: Religious Rhetoric at Walt Disney World* tackles each of these issues. It approaches the "creation" issues from the premise that Walt Disney and his company did not seem to flinch at the notion of holding both a Scientific Realist position and a Christian Realist position, simultaneously. Furthermore, I demonstrate that—apart from their removal of God from the picture—Scientific Realists can be easily accommodated within the interpretive possibilities in the Bible. It is possible for a Scientific Realist to be simultaneously a Christian Realist, if s/he **follows the gauntlet I laid down.** In short, if the Scientific Realist accepts the "presumption" that the Bible is true unless and until proven false, s/he can and will continue, simultaneously, to be a Christian Realist.

On page 4 of *Disneology*, I point out:

> Disney was a huge fan of President **Abraham Lincoln**. Lincoln is the president who receives the greatest attention in the "Hall of Presidents" at the Magic Kingdom . . . Lincoln asserts that all men are "**created**" equal. He identifies the Declaration of Independence as the "**truth**." . . . Mention of the "creator" in the Declaration of Independence is reiterated in the "American Adventure" in EPCOT.

Yet, on page 5, I continue:

> The "Universe of Energy" attraction at EPCOT presents the origins of the universe from a wholly god-less perspective. The perspective of **physics** informs riders that originally, there was a "big bang" in which a great amount of energy was converted

into huge supplies of mass. ... The perspective of **Geology** (the study of the Earth) then takes over. This originally very hot planet was a fiery, molten, and gaseous mixture. The gasses surrounded the planet until the planet cooled; then, water condensed onto the surface of the earth and became the seas. (Not too many years ago ... WDW had corroborated these views of physics and geology in a preshow to "The Living Seas" exhibit. Again, no mention of a creator was to be found.) The perspective of **Evolutionary Biology** is/was presented in both the Energy and Seas shows, as plant life is followed by water life, then amphibian life, etc.

THE EVOLUTION ISSUE

In my book *Disneology*: *Religious Rhetoric at Walt Disney World* (p. 55), I comment: "The most stressful and emotionally divisive debate between scientists and theologians is over the issue of evolution." For those who are not inclined to accept any semblance of evolution, those who believe that any evolutionary explanation of biological existence is counter to the Bible, I offer the following encouragement (p. 57):

> Believers in gradual evolution have been hoping that the study of fossils (paleontology) will yield scientific evidence of the various transitional stages of development each genus and species went through as it evolved. They are searching for "missing links." The website AllAboutScience.org (http://www.allaboutscience.org/missing-link-faq.htm) reports:
>
>> Stephen J. Gould, America's most famous evolutionist . . . stated, "The extreme rarity of transitional forms in the fossil record persists as the trade secret of paleontology. The evolutionary . . . textbooks have data only at the tips and nodes of their branches; the rest is

> inference, however reasonable, not the evidence of fossils. I wish in
> no way to impugn the potential validity of gradualism. I wish only
> to point out that it was never seen in the rocks."

Nevertheless, for those who would dismiss the Bible because they are persuaded by the evolutionary argument, I submitted also the following (pp. 57-58):

> Genesis 1:11 indicates "how" God made plants. He SPOKE to the land: "Let the land produce vegetation." Genesis 1:12 confirms: "The land produced vegetation." One way of viewing this phenomenon is to say that God delegated to land the capacity for producing plant life. . . . In a somewhat similar manner (but with a curious departure in the way it is phrased), in Genesis 1:20, God SPOKE to the waters: "Let the waters teem with living creatures." . . . Water animal life was the first level of animal life. . . . In Genesis 1:24, we return to a formula similar to the formula for making plants. God SPOKE to the land: "Let the land produce living creatures." If God delegated to land the capacity for producing plant life, and then (later) the capacity for producing living creatures, it may be that once God created elemental animal life (in the waters), the land was given the capacity for developing that animal life. In other words, there appears to be some room for a somewhat theologically-based evolution/gradualism theory.

THE HUMAN ISSUE

Genesis, however, does NOT say that God SPOKE humans into existence. On pages 58-59 of *Disneology*, I observe:

Genesis 1:27 states: "God created man in his own image . . . male and female created He them." Genesis 2:7 adds the detail that God formed man from the dust of the ground and breathed into his nostrils the breath of life before man became a living being. . . . The term "create" is used by Genesis only in terms of creating the "heavens and the earth" in 1:1 . . . creating "the great creatures of the sea and every living" thing in the sea in 1:21 (the beginning of animal life), and God creating "man in his own image" in 1:27. . . . [A]ll creation seems to have been accomplished by God "speaking," with the lone exception of the creation of Adam.

To the matter of what it means to be in the "image of God," I devote several chapters of *Disneology* (Chapters 10-15). My observations on the senses in which man is unique from all other animals are not the musings of a theologian; rather, they are the observations of a Twentieth Century (agnostic) genius in the field of Communication, Kenneth Burke. Burke asserts that the human is the symbol-using (symbol-making) animal. Skeptics are hard-pressed to find any other animal species that "creates" or "makes" its own communication, as does the human. Since God, in Genesis, also creates/makes, human communication is effectively an image of God. Burke asserts that since the human is the only animal capable of using the hortatory negative (Thou shalt not!), and since the hortatory negative is the basis of morality, the human is "moralized" by the negative. Morality makes the human into the image of God. Burke asserts that the human is the "tool-making, tool-using" animal. Other animals may use tools that are found in nature or created by man, but humans (using symbolicity) technically make and use their own tools. They are, thus, separated from their natural condition by instruments of their own making. This "creative" nature is, again, the image of God. Burke asserts that humans are goaded by a "spirit of hierarchy." His use of the word "spirit" here is akin to his use of "symbol-making." While other animals have natural, instinctive, hierarchies (back-biting for wolves, pecking order for chickens, etc.), humans symbolically create zillions of hierarchies. This creative function, along with the hierarchal element evident in all creation, makes humans the image of God. Burke asserts that the human is "rotten with perfection." He is not saying that the human is, by any means, perfect—just that he has an innate notion of what perfection means in many situations. This is also the image of God. The Dedication of my book *Implicit Rhetoric: Kenneth Burke's Extension of Aristotle's Concept of Entelechy* reads: "To God, the Ultimate Symbol-User."

THE *HOMO SAPIENS*/NEANDERTHAL ISSUE

According to the Smithsonian Institute website http://humanorigins.si.edu/evidence/human-fossils/species/homo-sapiens, human evolution researchers/paleoanthropologists admit that they still do not know: "Who was our direct evolutionary ancestor? Was it *Homo heidelbergensis,* like many paleoanthropologists think, or another species? . . . [or] How much interbreeding occured between our species and *Homo neanderthalensis?*" In other words, it is clear that *Homo sapiens* is a separate "species," originating thousands, not millions, of years ago. That some interbreeding between the Homo sapiens and the (older and extinct species) Neanderthals occurred is accepted by paleoanthropologists: According to Charles Q. Choi, "Why Neanderthals Likely Fathered Few Kids with Modern Humans," *Live Science* [http://www.livescience.com/54359-neanderthal-y-chromosome-caused-miscarriages.html]:

Humans today often carry around a small chunk of DNA from Neanderthals, suggesting we interbred with our closest known extinct relatives at some point in our history. So why isn't there more Neanderthal DNA in modern humans? Turns out, the Y chromosome may have been key in keeping the two lineages apart by creating conditions that might often have led to miscarriages if or when the two got together, researchers now say.

The very point that the two species were separate species and that interbreeding was a rare and difficult possibility suggest that *Homo sapiens* was a distinct creation. But what about the Bible and God making man "in His own image"? Doesn't the very existence of Neanderthal, Heidelberg, Floresiensis, Erectus, Rudolfensis, and Habilis fossils disprove that notion? In my forthcoming book *Angels and demons: The personification of communication*, I address the issue of the marriages in Genesis 6 between the "sons of God" and the "daughters of man," drawing on the suggested interbreeding between Neanderthals and *Homo sapiens*, while at the same time considering the Hebrew language:

> Genesis 1:26 quotes God: "Let us make man INTO our image." The Hebrew consonant (ב) that I have translated "into" is typically translated "in." Nevertheless, "into" is a perfectly legitimate translation. . . . Due to the . . . fossil record that seems to provide evidence of the existence of a non-symbol-using version of man that predates the symbol-using variety, a translation of "into" . . . could accommodate such evidence. In other words, a possibility exists that God originally made a man . . . who did not have symbol-using capacities. He could not speak a language, make tools, paint pictures on cave walls, etc. Then, at some point, God made the same type of being WITH symbol-using capacities (i.e., with

His image: He created Adam). . . . The sons of God, in this scenario, would be the offspring of Adam—those who were created "with" [or "made into"] God's image, and hence, could be thought of as his "sons." The daughters of men, in this scenario, would be the female offspring of the purely "animal" man, the Neanderthals or some such. . . . What would happen if one bred a very intelligent (. . . son of God) man with a very physically adapted (. . . daughter of man) woman? Would their offspring not have the capability of being "heroes" and "men of name?"

My point is not that one must accept the preceding explanation/interpretation, but only that the Hebrew text is capable of one or more interpretations that could accommodate the views of paleoanthropologists. THE BIBLE IS TRUE, UNLESS AND UNTIL IT IS PROVEN FALSE.

THE BIG BANG ISSUE

In *Disneology* (pp. 31-34), I point out:

> "Big Bang," Einstein's E=MC², Aristotle's HULĒ, Disney's Universe of Energy, and Kenneth Burke's Logology all converge. . . . According to Einstein, Mass (or Aristotle's HULĒ) can be changed into Energy, and vice versa. Einstein explains his theory of relativity, as follows:
>
>> It followed from the special theory of relativity that mass and energy are both but different manifestations of the same thing -- a somewhat unfamiliar conception for the average mind. Furthermore, the equation E is equal to m c-squared, in which energy is put equal to mass, multiplied by the square of the velocity of light, showed that very small amounts of mass may be converted into a very large

amount of energy and vice versa. The mass and energy were in fact equivalent, according to the formula mentioned above. This was demonstrated by Cockcroft and Walton in 1932, experimentally.

. . . The Big Bang theory of the origins of the universe is based on the notion that "in the beginning" there was a huge conversion of Energy into Mass—a Big Bang. But what was the source of this tremendous supply of Energy? Theological answer: God. Even more specifically, for John, the energy present in the spoken Word of God. . . . This view . . . supplies an important answer for adherents of the Big Bang Theory that physics . . . [does] not supply—the source of the tremendous supply of Energy that was converted into Mass.

THE AGE OF THE UNIVERSE ISSUE

In *Disneology* (pp. 25-28), I comment:

Certainly, it is possible to interpret the Genesis account of creation as stating that the entire universe and its inhabitants (up to and including humans) were completely created in six twenty-four-hour periods, just a few thousand years ago. This translation is possible because the word "day" (YOM, in the Hebrew) most frequently refers to "one twenty-four-hour period. . . . unless the term day/YOM can mean something other than a twenty-four-hour period." . . . In addition to the twenty-four-hour denotation, the word YOM also, at times, simply means "light," as opposed to "darkness" (Genesis 1:5).

YOM also refers to time periods other than the twenty-four-hour variety. In the first chapter of Genesis, God created man—both male and female—and gave them instructions to multiply and fill the Earth, all in one YOM (Day Six). In the second chapter, there is an expanded discussion of several steps in this process. First, God creates Adam, a male, and instructs him to keep the Garden of Eden, to name the animals, to refrain from eating of the Tree of the Knowledge of Good and Evil, etc. Then, God . . . brings a deep sleep upon him, removes a rib from his side, fashions it into a female (Eve), and brings her to Adam. Later (when Adam and Eve are not together), a serpent successfully induces Eve to eat from the Tree, and Eve subsequently successfully tempts Adam to do so. They invent clothing and hide from God. God discovers them and interrogates them. They are cast from the Garden of Eden and FINALLY told to be fruitful and multiply in the Earth. These are quite a few events to have all been completed in one twenty-four-hour period. Nevertheless, Genesis 5:1-2 confirms that Adam and Eve were created in a YOM.

Consider another example of YOM lasting longer than twenty-four hours. In Genesis 2:17, God tells Adam that "in the day you eat" from the Tree of Knowledge of Good and Evil, you shall surely die. Since (according to Genesis 5:8) Adam lived 930 years, the YOM in which he ate and died appears to be quite long. In fact, this nearly-one-thousand-year-long YOM appears to be close to the famous formula found in Psalm 90:4: "For a thousand years are in [God's] eyes as a YOM . . ." Changing the Hebrew word YOM/day to the Greek term HEMERA/day, Second Peter 3:8 (KJV) declares: "One day with the Lord is as a thousand years, and a thousand years is as one day."

. . . A third example of YOM lasting longer than twenty-four hours is found in Genesis 2:4. This verse seems to suggest that ALL of creation—heavens, Earth, plants, animals, and humans—occurred in a single YOM! Even those who suggest that God created all things in 144 hours are hesitant to assert that it all happened within 24 hours.

While sound Biblical scholarship certainly permits the interpretation that the heavens and Earth and all varieties of inhabitants were formed in 144 hours, this is not the ONLY possible interpretation . . .

Furthermore, the first word of the Bible has [possibly] been mistranslated. The first word of the Bible in the original language of Hebrew is BERESHIT. It is almost always translated: "In the beginning." There is, however, a problem with that translation. The problem lies in the fact that the term BERESHIT is a Hebrew "construct" form. This means that the term "Beginning" should be connected with another noun by the word "of." The second word of Genesis is NOT, however, a noun; it is the word BARA', a verb, translated as "He created." . . . It [also] is quite permissible [by changing vowel pointings] . . . to read BARA' as a noun (or Gerund): "the creating." This is how the translation of Genesis 1:1-2 might, thus, read: "In the Beginning of God's creating the heavens and the Earth, the Earth was formless and void."

If the translation just offered is true, we do not know for certain exactly where the Genesis creation account begins. What is the exact point in the beginning of creating that the first day described in Genesis actually begins? It's somewhere in the beginning, but the Earth is apparently already in existence, albeit in a formless and chaotic state. Of course, this is not the ONLY possible translation/interpretation of Genesis 1:1-2, but NEITHER is the translation: "In the beginning God created the heavens and the Earth."

THE CHRONOLOGY OF THE SUN ISSUE

I note, on page 43 of *Disneology*: "The order of Creation in Genesis mirrors the order of the origins of the universe as depicted by science in Disney's Epcot exhibits." Nevertheless, some take issue with the introduction by Genesis of the sun, moon and stars on Day Four. This, they assert, is out of order in the origin of the universe. Contrarily, I point out (pp. 45-46):

The Bible does not say plants were "created" before the sun, moon, and stars. The term "create" is used by Genesis only in terms of creating the "heavens and the earth" in 1:1 (which seems to imply [in the term "heavens"] that the Sun, Moon, and stars were already created by Day One), creating "the great creatures of the sea and every living" thing in the sea in 1:21 (the beginning of animal life), and God creating "man in his own image" in 1:27. The Bible only implies that on the 4th day, the sun, moon, and stars were made visible in the firmament, to divide day from night. On the implication of "visibility" in Day 4, what else could lights dividing day from night, being markers for seasons, days, and years, and shedding light upon the earth be? This chronological issue of when the Sun, Moon, and stars came into being seems to be the only serious objection non-believers cite regarding the order of creation in the first chapter of Genesis. Disney's exhibits provide a visual tour of prehistory: The big bang happens, the earth is hot, there is light (from the hot magma and volcanoes) and the "waters" are so hot, they are nothing but vapors surrounding the earth so dense that no light from sun-moon-stars is visible, the earth starts to cool, water vapors begin to condense and gather into seas, vegetation begins, and finally the condensation is so thorough the sun-moon-stars are visible from the surface of the earth. The point I am making has to do with the fact that, at some time prior to the sun-moon-stars becoming visible from the surface of the earth, the earth's waters were in a gaseous form, hovering above the land surfaces. We know that these water vapors, if they were suspended above the surface of the Earth in gaseous form would be impenetrable by sunlight since we can see that, after they condensed and became the sea, we need only go below the surface of the sea a few thousand feet before we encounter absolute darkness.

The now-discontinued Disney pre-show film of the Living Seas (replicating the order described by physicists) shows this exact order—with vegetation beginning to grow PRIOR TO the emergence of the visibility of sun, moon, and stars. For further reading on creation issues, I refer you to my book *Disneology: Religious Rhetoric at Walt Disney World*.

Creation issues are extremely important for Christian Realists. If even the Ten Commandments assert that God created, and with much of the theology in both testaments predicated on the Genesis account of Creation and Adam and Eve, how could any Christian dismiss these issues as unimportant? Along with issues of the end of time in Revelation and the New Testament mini-apocalypses, and with questions about the reliability of the Gospel accounts, Creation issues are the front lines of the war. Regarding creation issues (and the other issues), the Bible is true until proven false.

Chapter 14

The PAROUSIA is True until Proven False

One of the premises on which the Logic of Christianity is founded is the argument that Jesus fulfilled multiple Old Testament prophecies (see the Gospel accounts). So, what about Jesus' own prophecies, regarding his "Coming" (aka, the PAROUSIA)? According to a Pew Research poll published August 24, 2016, the majority of individuals (78%) who now say that they have no religion were actually raised in religious families. Furthermore, "About half of current religious 'nones' [this phrase means: those who now say that they have no religion] who were raised in a religion (49%) indicate that a lack of belief led them to move away from religion." Prominent among those issues that led to a lack of belief were "learning about evolution when [they] went away to college" and "lack of any sort of scientific or specific evidence of a creator." That is why I focused the previous chapter on the truth of "Creation." I believe the Creation issue is unquestionably essential to the Logic of Christianity. Having been an active member for nearly fifty years of the extremely critical academic society—The Society of Biblical Literature—I have been exposed to the onslaught of negative biblical scholarship. I have concluded (as I mentioned at the close of my last chapter): "Along with issues of the end of time apocalypses, and with questions about the historicity of the Gospel accounts, Creation issues are the front lines of the war."

In this chapter and the next, I turn to "issues of the PAROUSIA of Christ and the end of time in Paul, Revelation, and the Gospel mini-apocalypses." Jesus is reported in the Gospels to have predicted that his PAROUSIA [often, incorrectly I think, called the "Second Coming"] would occur within a generation:

1. In Matthew 16:28 (KJV), Jesus predicts: "[T]here shall be some standing here, which shall not taste of death, till they see the Son of Man coming (ERCHOMAI) in his kingdom." This appears to place a serious time limit for the fulfillment of Jesus' PAROUSIA prophecy. In the parallel accounts, Mark 9:1, using a different grammatical form of ERCHOMAI, offers the additional detail that this coming would be in "power." Luke 9:27 doesn't mention a specific "coming" of Jesus, but states that they will see the "kingdom of God." Scholars have interpreted Luke's phraseology as an attempt to "delay the ESCHATON." ESCHATON is a word meaning "the End." These scholars are suggesting that, by the time Luke wrote his Gospel, the church was beginning to back away from a belief that Jesus would return within decades of his Resurrection. But why would Luke (more clearly than the other two evangelists) spell out exactly a time frame for the appearance of the kingdom of God: "when you see

Jerusalem compassed with armies" (Luke 21:20 [KJV], a clear reference to the war on Jerusalem that began in 68 A.D., within the "lifetime" of some who heard Jesus' prophecy)?

2. Paul, writing in I Corinthians 15, verses 51 and 52 (KJV) corroborates the expectation that Jesus' PAROUSIA would happen within the lifetime of some first generation Christians: "[51] Behold, I shew you a mystery; We shall not all sleep, but we shall all be changed, [52] In a moment, in the twinkling of an eye, at the last trump: for the trumpet shall sound, and the dead shall be raised incorruptible, and we shall be changed." Scholars agree that Paul (by using the term "we" in all three instances) is expecting the PAROUSIA within either his lifetime or the lifetime of his contemporaries. Earlier in this chapter (15:23), Paul previews what he expands on in the verses just cited: "For as in Adam all die, even so in Christ shall all be made alive. But every man in his own order: Christ the firstfruits; afterward they that are Christ's at his coming (PAROUSIA)." Paul wrote his epistles before the Gospels were written down. Clearly, an expectation of an early PAROUSIA of Christ was pervasive in the Early Church.

3. Combine these predictions of the PAROUSIA occurring within the lifetime of Jesus' contemporaries with the several statements to the effect that Jesus' contemporary "generation" (KJV) would not pass until his PAROUSIA had occurred (Matthew 23:36 and 24:34, Mark 13:30, Luke 21:32). Of the three Synoptic Gospels, only Matthew (24:3, 27, 37, and 39) employs the term PAROUSIA (as does Paul) to name what all

three gospels describe as "the Son of man coming (ERCHOMENON) in the cloud/s with power and glory." Revelation 1:7 agrees that he is coming on the clouds.

4. The amount of time required for the accomplishment of the actual event called PAROUSIA to occur, however, seems to be negligible. Even though the Synoptic Gospels speak of seeing Jesus "coming in the clouds," which could suggest a "noticeable" length of time, Matthew 24:27 suggests the time frame of the PAROUSIA to be as "lightning" going from the east to the west. Matthew 24:39-41 offers a glimpse of two men in the field or two women at the mill—one taken and the other left—something that seems to imply a split-second disappearance. As cited earlier, Paul, in I Corinthians 15:52 suggests a split-second PAROUSIA: "In a moment, in the twinkling of an eye."

5. John, the author of Revelation, writing in 69 A.D., (within the "lifetime" of some who heard Jesus' prophecy), indicates that the time is "near" or "short" for the fulfilling of the apocalyptic prophecies (Revelation 1:3, 12:12). Jesus repeatedly states: "I am coming (ERCHOMAI) quickly" (Revelation 3:11, 22:7, 12, and 20).

6. It is true that some New Testament books, such as James and II Peter acknowledge the impatient frustrations of some in their audiences that Jesus' PAROUSIA has not yet occurred. James 5:7-8 (KJV) states:

> [7] Be patient therefore, brethren, unto the coming of the Lord. Behold, the husbandman waiteth for the precious fruit of the earth, and hath long

patience for it, until he receive the early and latter rain. [8] Be ye also patient; stablish your hearts: for the coming of the Lord draweth nigh.

James not only reasserts the predicted coming, but also states that it is "drawing near." II Peter 3:4 (KJV) addresses the point:

> Where is the promise of his coming? for since the fathers fell asleep, all things continue as they were from the beginning of the creation. . . . [8] But, beloved, be not ignorant of this one thing, that one day is with the Lord as a thousand years, and a thousand years as one day. [9] The Lord is not slack concerning his promise, as some men count slackness; but is longsuffering to us-ward, not willing that any should perish, but that all should come to repentance.

7. The strongest argument critical scholars have for suggesting that New Testament Christianity abandoned hope in a PAROUSIA that would occur within the generation to whom Jesus prophesied it is to claim that New Testament books, such as Luke and Revelation, were written well after the time of first generation Christians. While that position has been advanced by some critical scholars, it is by no means proven. For example, while many critical scholars want to date the writing of Revelation at 96 A.D., I point out in my book *Revelation: The Human Drama* (Lehigh University Press, 2001, p. 37):

According to (an apparently private conversation with) John A. T. Robinson, [the renowned British scholar, F. F.] Bruce "now inclines" in the direction of the earlier date [69 A.D.]. Robinson's own thesis is that Revelation (and all other New Testament books) should be redated prior to 70 A.D. Robert M. Grant . . . criticizes Robinson's work . . . Yet, Grant is only critiquing Robinson's book--he is not disavowing the possibility that the date of Revelation was prior to 70. Robinson even cites Grant as allowing for the possibility of an early date for Revelation: "Grant, INT, 237, is prepared to say 'a situation between 68 and 70 is not excluded.'"

If one redates "all . . . New Testament books . . . prior to 70 A.D.," there is absolutely no proof in the New Testament that the prophesied PAROUSIA did not occur. On the contrary, if all New Testament books were written prior to 70 A.D., there is a missing link between the New Testament church and the Early Catholic Church. Indeed, renowned church historian S. G. F. Brandon, in his book *The Fall of Jerusalem and the Christian Church* (London: S.P.C.K., 1957), claims that any record of the church existing virtually disappears for a period of twenty years after 70 A.D. What happened to the Christians?

8. In my book on Revelation, page 36, I observe:

> Elisabeth Schüssler Fiorenza claims that "New Testament scholars generally agree that the author of Revelation [was writing] . . . at the end of the first century." But this consensus is mistaken. If this general consensus view were correct, presumably the intended audience would be primarily gentile in makeup. [However,] R. H. Charles . . . contends

that the author of Revelation is Jewish and J. Massyngberde Ford questions whether or not the work is Christian at all, or a *thoroughly* Jewish book. If any portion of Ford's argument is accepted, what Fiorenza claims to be the consensus view regarding the date, and hence the intended audience of Revelation, needs to change. The Church at the end of the first century appears to be quite gentile in makeup. In this regard, S. G. F. Brandon notes:

> [T]he author of the Acts in his presentation of the tradition of Christian Origins never gives any indication that the numbers of the Gentile converts were large, while he makes several statements about the considerable numerical strength of the Jewish Christians in Palestine, which . . . must be fairly interpreted as genuine indications of the comparative situation.

Yet, Justin Martyr, writing in the second century at approximately 135 A.D., can have a debate with Trypho, the Jew, in a context that seems to clearly indicate the almost total absence of Jews in the Church!

What happened to the Jewish Christians?

9. In 1878, a British exegete named J. Stuart Russell published a book entitled *The Parousia.* Still in print (now, with a Foreword by Reformed leader R. C. Sproul), the author concludes, quite logically (p. 565):

> [T]he predictions of our Lord in Matt. xxiv . . . had a veritable accomplishment. . . . These predictions are bounded by certain limits of

time. The time is explicitly declared to fall within the period of the then

existing generation. . . . And why should it be thought incredible?

Russell anticipates that skeptics of his suggestion will offer an answer to the question

just asked: "Because there is no historical evidence of the fact." However, if such an

event were predicted to occur in a negligible length of time—such as "lightning" going

from the east to the west or "in a moment, in the twinkling of an eye," how could there

possibly be any historical evidence? The answer to that question, which J. Stuart

Russell reached in the 19th Century, is the (same) answer that I reached, entirely

independently of Russell, in the 21st Century: It's the twenty-year absence of the

evidence that a Church existed following the Jerusalem War of 66 to 73 A.D. It's the

fact that, once the Church reemerges, it is almost entirely Gentile; whereas, it had been

dominated by Jews in the New Testament period. Russell writes:

> The principal, if not the only, portion that seems to come within the
> cognizance of human sense, is the removal of a great multitude of the
> disciples of Christ from this earthly scene. . . . [T]here should be some
> trace in history of this sudden disappearance of so vast a body of
> believers. . . . a blank in history. . . . a failure, at the least, in the
> continuity of the records of Christianity. [T]he predictions do not
> require an absolute and universal removal of the *whole* body of the
> faithful (for it is manifest that there is a clear distinction made between
> the watchful and the unwatchful, the ready and the unready . . .).

Such a huge gap does exist, as seen by the church historians.

10. Does the historical gap in the records of the existence of the Church prove that the Church was raptured? No. That proposition could not possibly be proven, historically. But, it does argue the POSSIBILITY. Everything else in Jesus' prophecy occurred within a generation: The Temple was both profaned and destroyed; there were wars and rumors of war as the Roman Empire progressively attacked the Land of Israel; Christians were delivered up to councils and synagogues, and beaten, but gave their testimony before kings and governors.

The view that the PAROUSIA predicted by Jesus truly occurred sometime around 70 A.D., is not only my own view and that of J. Stuart Russell, but also (with variants) the view of the 16th Century Jesuit Catholic theologian, Luis del Alcázar and 17th Century Reformed exegete Hugo Grotius. F. F. Bruce observes: "Hugo Grotius (1583-1645) . . . was the first Reformed exegete to give up the identification of the Papacy with the Antichrist and he held that some of the visions of Rev[elation] reflect the period before, and others the period after, the fall of Jerusalem in A.D. 70." Bruce continues, "[Grotius] may thus be regarded as the pioneer of the literary-critical approach to the book [of Revelation]." No less than the most respected Revelation scholar of the 20th Century— R. H. Charles--indicates that Revelation should "be taken as referring first and chiefly to the times in which it was originally written." This assertion by Charles summarizes the position of the Contemporary-Historical methodology of interpreting Revelation. Along with the scholarly consensus, the Contemporary-Historical methodology is what I personally follow, even though I agree with Charles's earlier (69 A.D.) datings, but not his later (96 A.D.) datings. Unlike Charles (but like Russell and others), I suggest that the predictions of John regarding those times in which Revelation was originally written truly occurred. I offer evidence of that view in my book *Revelation: The Human Drama.* Merrill C. Tenney of Wheaton College refers to the view of R. H. Charles, which he calls the "view of the majority of liberal scholars," as the Preterist School of Revelation—that the book's symbolism "relates only to the events of the day in which it was written." It is with that view of the PAROUSIA—that it was predicted to happen within the generation of Jesus—that I am dealing in this chapter. It is the majority interpretation of critical scholars. Most of these critical scholars use this interpretation of the PAROUSIA prophecies to discredit the Bible and Jesus. They say that the PAROUSIA, while predicted, did not happen within the first generation. I am arguing that, if one offers the Bible the "presumption" of "truth"—that the Bible is true unless proven wrong—the truth of the Bible must stand. If the PAROUSIA was predicted to occur in a "moment," in the "twinkling of an eye," as a "lightning" flash, there is no way that it could be proven that it did not occur . . . UNLESS there is evidence that the whole church continued in existence uninterrupted from the day it began. BUT . . . there is evidence that the existence of the church WAS INTERRUPTED for about 20 years! Therefore, I conclude that the PAROUSIA very well may have happened around 70 A.D. I, therefore, continue to hold to the presumption of Biblical truth.

So, if the PAROUSIA has occurred (around 70 A.D.), what does the Bible say about the rest of human history? Revelation offers a very interesting sketch of the remainder of human history, a projection of history that has occurred with startling precision. The Battle of Armageddon is misunderstood; the Battle of Gog and Magog is yet to occur. It was not predicted to occur until after the thousand-year incarceration of the Dragon. What do these predictions mean? These issues will be the subject of my next chapter.

Chapter 15

Revelation is True until Proven False

As I was working on my Ph.D. thesis at Purdue University, analyzing the Book of Revelation from a Burkean standpoint, a scholar asked me: "Surely [in the 1990s], you don't still believe in predictive prophecy, do you?" The answer is: Yes, I do. This chapter is focused on demonstrating that Revelation's prophecies have been and are coming true. As I point out in my book *ArguMentor*,

> Miracles and fulfilled prophecies are proofs that do not necessarily rely on *ethos* [and, hence, are logical, relying on *logos*]. However, ACCOUNTS of miracles, absent substantiating evidence, do again rely on *ethos*. It is generally advisable in argumentation not to rely excessively on *ethos*, unless both parties in the dispute are willing to stipulate that the individual (or individuals) being relied on for *ethos* is in a position to know the truth of a matter.

How would one go about proving that Paul met Jesus via a BAT QOL, on the road to Damascus? How would one prove that he survived a venomous snakebite unscathed? How would one prove that Peter miraculously escaped from prison? How would one ever prove that Jesus was born of a virgin, or that he walked on water, changed water into wine, fed 5000 with two fish and five loaves of bread, raised Lazarus from the dead, and performed numerous healings? Conversely, how would one ever disprove those things? One must simply TRUST the person/s relating the account. Of course, in the case of the gospel accounts of miracles, apostles and eye witnesses were willing to die instead of recanting their testimonies—if one believes the "accounts" of their deaths. How would one prove (or disprove) these accounts?

Prophecies, on the other hand, can be tested; they are not substantially reliant on ETHOS. We have alluded to some of the prophecies from the Old Testament that point to the coming Christ/Messiah—prophecies that helped to prove Jesus' messiahship. I argued, in Chapter14: The PAROUSIA is True until Proven False, that Jesus' own major prophecy regarding the PAROUSIA should be given the presumption of truth. So, we now turn to the major book of prophecy in the New Testament to see if it may be given the same presumption of truth. In Revelation, John predicted: the PAROUSIA, a seven year war between the Beast and the harlot Babylon divided by two periods of 3 ½ years ("time, times, and half a time") each, the Fall of Babylon, the Battle of Armageddon, Casting the Beast and False Prophet into the Lake of Fire, Casting the Dragon— chained—into the Abyss for one thousand years, a corresponding thousand-year Reign of Christ and his Followers on Earth, the Release of the Dragon after the thousand years, the Rise of Gog and Magog, the Battle of Gog and Magog, Casting the Dragon into the Lake of Fire, the

Destruction of the Old Heavens and Old Earth, and the Creation of the New Heavens and the New Earth, inhabited by the New Jerusalem.

Before I begin to discuss the fulfillment of these prophecies, I begin with an internal summary of the syllogistic chain I have called the Logic of Christianity. We are nearing the conclusion of our presentation of the Logic of Christianity. If as:

1. Chapter 1 observes, "faith" is a logical continuum, stretching all the way from believing that something is "barely possible" to the firm conviction that something is "almost definitely" true, and as:

2. Chapter 2 argues that, in order to build "faith," we build (rhetorical/logical) arguments in terms of what Aristotle calls a "syllogistic chain," with one argument built on top of another, and as:

3. Chapter 3 argues, there have been four logical explosions in the history of man, and the Renaissance was the one that began to undo faith in Christianity—culminating in Modernism, which taught us to "doubt" everything (thus, opposing all religious faith)—but that Postmodernism (around 1950) taught us to "doubt" Modernism, thus, leaving us with "faith" in probable truth (and reviving the possibility of religious faith), and as:

4. Chapter 4 argues (as the 4th link in the syllogistic chain), the universe exists as a result of the "action" of an "agent," and as:

5. Chapter 5 argues, that an agent acted using the agency of LOGOS in the formation of the universe, being motivated by both a self-actualization purpose and a social purpose, and as:

6. Chapter 6 argues, the most "logical" contemporarily viable candidate for the agent who formed the universe is the one single god who is acknowledged as God by the world's three major world religions—Judaism, Christianity, and Islam—i.e., the God of Abraham, and as:

7. Chapter 7 argues, Christianity (of the three religions) best meets the Koranic suggestion that Abraham's son (whom God asked to be sacrificed) is to be replaced with a "great sacrifice," encompasses Isaiah's view that God has "no pleasure in the blood of bulls and lambs and goats," and further presents Jesus as Isaiah's suffering servant who was led to the slaughter like a lamb, and as:

8. Chapter 8 argues, Jesus' Transfiguration in the presence of at least one Immortal (Elijah) answers the logical need for proof that Jesus was perfect, and not punishable by death (the wages of sin), but by subsequently dying anyway, he paid the price for the sins of all of Adam's children, and as:

9. Chapter 9 argues, Jesus' Crucifixion was maximum justice for any sin known to mankind, not for Jesus' own actions, but for the actions of any human that has ever lived, and as:

10. Chapter 10 argues, Jesus' Resurrection completes the cosmic circle of the logic of eternal life that began with the very first man, Adam, and as:

11. Chapter 11 argues, there are no credible proofs that the Resurrection never happened, and as:

12. Chapter 12 argues, the most credible communication God ever made with man—in His own handwriting (the Ten Commandments)—claims that God created the universe, and as:

13. Chapter 13 argues, presumption demands that Creation is true until proven false, and as:

14. Chapter 14 argues, since Jesus is God's Son, and must not, therefore, be capable of making errors in his own prophecies, presumption demands that his prediction of the PAROUSIA is true until proven false, then we may turn to the rest of the Bible, to establish that the other parts are also true until proven false, and to establish that Christianity is a logical worldview.

So, now, we turn to the prophecies included in the major book of prophecy in the New Testament, Revelation. Did John, the author of Revelation, make huge mistakes, as some claim? Among the important Revelation scholars, Adela Yarbro Collins (*Crisis and Catharsis: The Power of the Apocalypse.* Philadelphia: Westminster, 1984) views Revelation historically as "something less than absolute bedrock." She tries to present Revelation as a "perceived crisis" discussion. She writes: "It is not because I believe that the author of Revelation was intentionally deceptive or that he was a psychopathic personality. It is rather because he was a human like the rest of us." Her historical quest leads her to a quite difficult position--an inconsistency. On the one hand, she cites external evidence for "a date [of writing] of about 95 or 96" under the reign of Domitian. On the other hand, she knows that "[t]here is insufficient evidence to warrant the conclusion that Domitian persecuted Christians as Christians." She points out that many interpreters see Revelation as a response to this situation: Domitian was persecuting Christians, even forcing them to worship the emperor. She says this entire scenario is false. Yarbro Collins claims the crisis addressed in Revelation is more perceived than real. This is frustrating. A more elaborate dramatistic analysis is possible if, as I suggested in the previous chapter, scholars revisit the dating of Revelation. More historical consistency may be found by dating the writing in 69 A.D. (which the Book of Revelation, itself, claims as a date of authorship). A more consistent and elaborate dramatistic analysis of Revelation is what my book (*Revelation: The Human Drama*) attempts to accomplish.

1. **John's Own Dating of the Book of Revelation.** Virtually every Revelation scholar weighs in on the claim that the seven or eight-headed beast of Revelation is Rome. The heads are kings. Five have fallen. In terms of dating the book, the book claims to be written during the reign of the sixth head. Hence, calculations ensue to determine the date of the book. It is difficult to see how the head count could begin before Julius Caesar. If Julius were head one, head six would be Nero who died in 68 A.D. Since Julius was never officially an emperor, it seems more likely that Augustus is head one, and that Galba who reigned only in 69 A.D. is head six. Since Tiberius was the first Emperor following Jesus birth, he might be head one in which case Otho who reigned only in 69 A.D. is head six. Skip Tiberius as head one and you have Vitellius who reigned only in 69 A.D. as head six. How many heads may be skipped before this clue of John's becomes meaningless? It appears that John is claiming that the book is being written around 69 A.D. There certainly

are elaborate ways of making Domitian equal head six, but it seems much easier to conclude that 69 A.D. is the date John claimed to write. Yarbro Collins is incorrect in dating the writing of Revelation in 95 or 96 A.D., according the Book of Revelation. She relies on the speculations of individuals who wrote much later than the cataclysmic events that Revelation predicts.

2. **The PAROUSIA.** Among the prophecies Revelation advances, this prophecy has already been considered somewhat. I commented in a previous chapter: "John, the author of Revelation, writing in 69 A.D., (within the 'lifetime' of some who heard Jesus' prophecy), indicates that the time is 'near' or 'short' for the fulfilling of the apocalyptic prophecies (Revelation 1:3, 12:12). Jesus repeatedly states: 'I am coming (ERCHOMAI) quickly' (Revelation 3:11, 22:7, 12, and 20). If John wrote Revelation in 69 A.D., and Jesus' PAROUSIA occurred sometime between 70 and 73 A.D., then the fulfillment of Jesus' Coming/PAROUSIA being near/short/quickly, from John's perspective, would be accurate indeed!

3. **Revelation and Daniel.** What I did not mention in the earlier chapter regarding Revelation and the PAROUSIA was the extent to which Jesus' own prophecies and John's Revelation prophecies tied themselves to the prophecies of Daniel. Revelation certainly has elements that are prophetic in the tradition of the Old Testament prophets. Jonah and Haggai may be the only Old Testament prophetic books not cited or alluded to in Revelation. John refers most frequently to the books of Daniel and Ezekiel, followed closely by Psalms, Isaiah, and Jeremiah.   Jesus is quoted in the gospels as alluding to a prophecy of Daniel

concerning an "abomination of desolation" that would be in control of the Temple in Jerusalem. The Gospel of Luke interprets the prophecy as a promise that armies would surround Jerusalem before the (then present) generation passed away." In the view of R. H. Charles, the first Beast of Revelation 13 "is the Roman Empire" which he equates with the fourth beast of Daniel. He further finds in a survey of Jewish and Christian exegetes from the Hellenistic period that "from 30 A.D. onwards Jewish exegesis universally and Christian exegesis generally took the Roman Empire to be the fourth kingdom in Daniel."

a. Daniel 9:24-27 speaks of seventy weeks of years pertaining to the coming of the Messiah/Christ. During the first sixty-nine weeks of years (483 years) from the decree to rebuild Jerusalem, the city--including its walls--would be rebuilt (9:25) and the messiah prince would be "cut off" (9:26). [A couple of such decrees to rebuild Jerusalem are recorded in history.] 1. If the starting point of Daniel's prophetic calculation was the decree of Cyrus recorded in Ezra 1:1-4, which occurred in 536 B.C., 483 years brings us to 53 B.C. 2. If the starting point was the decree of Artaxerxes recorded in Nehemiah 1 and 2, which occurred in 457 B.C., 483 years brings us to 26 A.D. Both of these dates approximate the lifetime of Jesus, so when Jesus (in Matthew 24:15), at approximately the year indicated by the Artaxerxes calculation, speaks of Daniel's "abomination of desolation" occurring in the future, he is effectively arguing that the Daniel prophecy is in the process of being fulfilled within the lifetime of his audience. In (Daniel 9:27) the last week of years, "a desolator on the wing of abominations" would come--a figure which Mark 13:14 identifies with Jesus' prediction of the fall of Jerusalem within a generation (Mark 13:30).   In the "middle" of that last week (the final seven years), the desolator (?)

"shall cause the offering and sacrifice to cease" (Daniel 9:27). Dividing the final seven years in the "middle" leaves two periods of "three and one-half years" each--one before the cessation of sacrifice and one following the cessation of sacrifice. Daniel concludes in 12:11 with the words: "And from the time the daily [sacrifice] shall be taken away, and the abomination that makes desolate set up, a thousand two hundred ninety days [= roughly, three and one-half years]," after which will come *qeytz* (a word which means "end" but is easily associated, for plays on words, with the verb "to awaken," cf. Ezekiel 7:6). The various interpretations of Daniel by Old Testament scholars need not be traced in this instance. The early church clearly interpreted Daniel in terms of the fall of Jerusalem. Thus, the reference to something happening in the middle of the last week of the seventy weeks of years is tantamount to the ultimate brink of the end (the PAROUSIA?). If the "great city which is spiritually called Sodom and Egypt, where also their lord was crucified" (Revelation 11:8) is an unmistakable reference to Jerusalem, as several scholars believe, the identification of the significance of Jerusalem's doom for John's audience is supported.

b. Syncretistic tendencies have been identified by Revelation scholars as the *porneia* (fornication) of which John accuses Jezebel and Babylon. Perhaps syncretistic tendencies are an important rationale in John's choosing "Babylon" as the name of the harlot. John appears to be greatly influenced by the book of Daniel. The heroes of Daniel are the young men who resist syncretism, once they have been carried away into "Babylon." They refuse to eat Babylonian food (Dan. 1:8) due to the presumption that they would be defiled

(SUMMOLUNÔ in the Septuagint [LXX]) by (the syncretistic? act of) eating the king's food. This is possibly the verse that John had in mind when he spoke in 14:4 of the "virgins" who were not defiled. John uses the cognate MOLUNÔ (defiled). The Babylonians attempt to assimilate the young men into their religion by renaming the young men with Babylonian names, often associated with Babylonian deities. Hananiah, Mishael, and Azariah are renamed respectively Shadrach, Meshach, and Aved Nego (Abednego). Daniel is renamed Belteshazzar. Daniel is determined to resist the law outlawing prayer to his God, even if it means incarceration with lions. The other three young heroes are determined to resist pagan worship, even if it means death in a fiery furnace. These heroes are models of anti-syncretism. Even John's literary style in many ways imitates this thoroughly anti-syncretistic book.

(Incidentally, Belteshazzar is a name that philologists cite as evidence for a later date for the book of Daniel, because the "t" should not be in the spelling. However, if the Jewish scribes who resisted syncretism added the "t" to the name Belshazzar in order to avoid the association of the hero Daniel with the Babylonian god, Bel, in the same way that the scribes added an extra "y" to Jerusalem, making it Yerushalayim, thus avoiding a pagan deity association, then the misspelling of Belshazzar is further evidence of an anti-syncretistic sentiment related to the book of Daniel.)

4. **Daniel and Revelation's Seven-Structure ("Time, Times, and Half a Time").** The language in Revelation 11:2-3, related to the "forty-two months" = "a thousand two hundred sixty days" (= three and one-half years) corresponds to Daniel 9 and the times of the destruction of Jerusalem and the temple. In fact, the "three and one-half years" of the

testimony of the Witnesses (11:3) and the "three and one-half years" of the trampling of the city by the Gentiles (11:2) have overwhelming significance themselves. They appear to be either one or both halves of the "last week of years" described by Daniel in chapter 9. The historical fact that the Jewish-Roman War from 66 to 73 A.D. lasted an exact SEVEN YEARS (or in Daniel's terminology a final "week of years") which occurred within the same generation as Jesus' audience, when he predicted the PAROUSIA, and which was constantly filled with "wars and rumors of wars" (Mark 13:7), and which concluded in two segments of "time, times, and half a time," from John's Revelation prophecy, there is stunning accuracy to support the prophecies of Daniel, Jesus, and John.

5. **Babylon (Jerusalem) is Fallen!** Yarbro-Collins is wrong, not only in her dating the writing of Revelation, but also in her identification of Babylon as Rome. The execution of Jesus had been accomplished by means of an alliance between the Jewish High Priestly party and the local representatives of the Roman Empire--Herod Antipas and Pontius Pilate. It was common knowledge among Jewish leaders that the High Priestly family was indebted to Herod's family for its prestige and power. Antipas' father, Herod the Great, had deposed the then-current (Hasmonean) High Priestly family in the years preceding Jesus' birth. In its place Herod (the Great) had installed a High Priest from among the Jews of the Babylonian Diaspora (those Jews who had been "carried away" into Babylon in the sixth century B.C. and who had not yet returned to Palestine). It is probable that the term "Babylon" in Revelation and I Peter is a code word for this High Priestly family and/or Jerusalem, the city controlled by the (Babylonian?) High Priestly family. Yarbro Collins

argues that John's use of the term Babylon provides evidence for a later date. Unfortunately, her reasoning is circular. She points out, "Most commentators agree that 'Babylon' . . . is a symbolic name for Rome." This is circular reasoning, since most commentators also place the date of writing at 96 A.D. To her credit, Yarbro Collins observes: "Most of the occurrences of Babylon as a symbolic name for Rome in Jewish literature are in the Apocalypse of Ezra . . ., the Syriac Apocalypse of Baruch . . ., and the fifth book of the *Sibylline Oracles*. . . . [T]he context makes it abundantly clear . . . Rome is called Babylon because her forces, like those of Babylon at an earlier time, destroyed the temple and Jerusalem." This is an interesting and valuable observation which pertains to the interpretation of the term Babylon. But, in her greatest use of circular reasoning, Yarbro Collins concludes, "It is highly unlikely that the name would have been used before the destruction of the temple by Titus. This internal evidence thus points decisively to a date after 70 C.E." Has Yarbro Collins completely missed the point (she personally implied) that since Babylon is never associated in Revelation with "destroy[ing] the temple and Jerusalem," Babylon in Revelation is not Rome? Babylon in Revelation is called a harlot. J. Massyngberde Ford points out, "The harlot . . . is also a Jewish OT theme depicting Jerusalem . . . and there is no clear indication that Babylon is Rome as in the Christian Sibyllines." If, as Ford understands, the harlot Babylon is faithless Jerusalem, John is continuing his rejection of the villains' nomenclature. Thus, he renames "the holy city" (11:2) in which the "Lord was crucified" (11:8), "Sodom and Egypt." If he refers to Jews who dwell in Judea, he calls them the "inhabitants of the land" and leaves off the words "of Israel" (in the same way that the "inhabitants of the land" in Genesis 34:30,

50:11, Numbers 14:14, 32:17, 33:52, 33:55, Joshua 2:9, 7:9, 9:24, Judges 1:33, etc., refers not to the Israelites, but to the pagan inhabitants of the land of Israel).

- Revelation 17:6 identifies Babylon as being "drunk from the blood of the saints and from the witnesses [*martus*] of Jesus." Revelation 18:24 claims that "in her was found the blood of the prophets and of the saints, and of all those having been slain on the earth/land." The only specific city accused elsewhere in the New Testament of "killing the prophets" is Jerusalem (Matt. 23:29-39; Lk. 11:47-51; 13:33-34). In the Old Testament, Ezekiel 22:2ff. calls Jerusalem the "city of bloodshed" who "brings on herself doom by shedding blood."

- Ezekiel 16:13 calls Jerusalem "a queen." In Revelation 18:7, Babylon calls herself a "queen." Both are actually harlots, according to their respective "prophets."

- Isaiah 50:1 and Jeremiah 3:8 speak of God giving Jerusalem/Israel/Judah a certificate of divorce. Ford argues that the scroll with seven seals is a specific type of bill of divorce used at the time (Ford, 92-94). The progressive opening of these seven seals, as God progressively moves towards divorcing Babylon/Jerusalem is described in Revelation chapters 5-11.

- In Ezekiel 16:29, Jerusalem increased her harlotry to "Babylonia, a land of merchants." In Revelation 18:3, the kings of the earth/land commit *porneia* with Babylon and the merchants of the earth became rich with her.

- Jeremiah 4:16 speaks of armies coming to destroy Jerusalem. Jeremiah 6:1 urges people to "Flee from Jerusalem." In Revelation 18:4, God's people are warned to "come out of her."

- Ezekiel 16:37ff. warns Jerusalem the harlot that all of her lovers will gather against her and strip her naked. Revelation 17:16 reports that the ten horns of the beast "will hate the harlot and will make her desolated [*erêmoô*] and naked and will eat her flesh and will burn her with fire."

- Not only will Babylon be left desolated in the previous verse, but also in 18:16 and 19. Likewise, the Septuagint/LXX of Daniel 9:27 leaves Jerusalem "desolated," and Matthew 24:15, predicting the destruction of Jerusalem, refers to Daniel's abomination of desolation, at which point Jesus urges those in Judea to "flee."

6. **The Battle of Armageddon.** During the years immediately preceding the destruction of the temple, John refers to Jerusalem as "Sodom and Egypt, where also their Lord was crucified" (Revelation 11:8). In this period, John writes of "the slander of those who say they are Jews and are not, but are a synagogue of Satan" (2:9). At this time, John calls Jerusalem "the harlot Babylon" (as J. M. Ford interprets) and exults in her gory destruction. Since John cannot refer to the Battle of Jerusalem, he gives the battle a new name: Armageddon. The word Armageddon is translated into the Greek from the Hebrew HAR MƏGIDDÔ (הר מגידו). The word HAR is translated into English as "mountain." The word MƏGIDDÔ is spelled in the Greek translation (LXX) of II Chronicles exactly as it is

spelled in Revelation. Here is the account of the Battle of Megiddo from II Chronicles 35:20-25:

> After all this, when Josiah had set the temple in order, Neco king of Egypt came up to make war at Carchemish on the Euphrates, and Josiah went out to engage him. But Neco sent messengers to him, saying, "What have we to do with each other, O King of Judah? I am not coming against you today but against the house with which I am at war, and God has ordered me to hurry. Stop for your own sake from interfering with God who is with me, so that He will not destroy you." However, Josiah would not turn away from him, but disguised himself in order to make war with him; nor did he listen to the words of Neco from the mouth of God, but came to make war on the plain of Megiddo. The archers shot King Josiah, and the king said to his servants, "Take me away, for I am badly wounded." So his servants took him out of the chariot and carried him in the second chariot which he had, and brought him to Jerusalem where he died and was buried in the tombs of his fathers.

Note, however, that Megiddo is not a mountain—but a plain. The only mountain associated with the Battle of Megiddo is Mount Zion (or Jerusalem) where Josiah died. John is continuing to refuse to refer to Jerusalem as Jerusalem or Mount Zion (a term he uses to refer to the 144,000 Christians). So, he refers to Mount Zion as Mount Megiddo. The Battle of Armageddon took place from 66 to 73 A.D. Jerusalem was annihilated (just as Josiah was killed and his kingdom was destroyed in 609 B.C.). Revelation is true in its prediction in 69 A.D. that Babylon the Great (understand: Jerusalem) would fall **near/short/quickly.**

7. The Destruction of the Beast and the False Prophet in the Lake of Fire. What is the Lake of Fire? For many individuals, it is just a synonym for Hell. But, most don't realize that, before Revelation, no one ever spoke or wrote of a Lake of Fire. John coined the phrase. For John, as for other Jews of his generation, a concept of a whole from which parts spring up and to which they return is the concept of the Nehar di-Nur (the "stream of fire"). This is not quite yet, however, a "lake of fire." Louis Ginzberg states: "Thus there are angels who spring up daily out of the stream Dinur (='stream of fire'; comp. Dan. 7.10); they praise God, and then disappear. Out of every word uttered by God angels are created." Is John familiar with the "stream of fire"? He does not mention this stream, but he describes a "lake of fire" into which the Devil and his angels are thrown. I believe that not only is John familiar with the "stream of fire," he even adds a twist to the concept: A stream keeps on flowing, but a "lake" is the end of the line. (The Lake does not allow water or fire to flow out of it; if something or someone is cast into the "lake" of fire, it will never ever reemerge.) Later Jewish writers speak of souls passing through the river of fire where "the wicked" are "judged." Whether these Jewish writers originated the idea of a river of fiery judgment or picked up on John's "lake of fire" is uncertain, but their concept does seem to demonstrate the ease with which fiery judgment and the stream of fire may be connected. The stream of fire is a magma anecdote--the whole in which God's "words" exist in their "essential" nature before and after becoming "angels" (= parts). In Revelation 19:19, the kings of the earth assemble for war with the Messiah/Christ, after the harlot (=Babylon=Jerusalem) has been destroyed, and the Beast is at that point thrown into the lake of fire. Remember the seven heads of the Beast who were seven kings: Beginning with the first in the Caesarean family, Julius Caesar, if Julius were head one, head six would be Nero who died in 68 A.D. The seventh head (currently reigning as John wrote) would be Galba who reigned only in 69 A.D. or Otho who reigned only in 69 A.D. or Vitellius who reigned only in 69 A.D. Vespasian who became emperor after these 3 short-lived emperors in 69 A.D. was the eighth head—Nero come back to life! Caird comments:

> Since the main trait of the monster's character is that it wages war on God's people, the emperor who best fits the specifications is Nero. His suicide in A.D. 68 could have been regarded as a deadly wound. . . . Only with the accession of Vespasian did the monster come to life again.

Vespasian was Nero's general whom Nero sent to besiege Jerusalem, and who in 69 A.D. became emperor after the Roman civil war which followed Nero's suicide (in 68 A.D.). With Caird, I find Vespasian to be the best candidate for the head which "seemed to have had a fatal wound, but the fatal wound had been healed" (Revelation 13:3 [NIV]). No other candidate for emperor could more clearly have represented Nero-returned-to-life to the Jews in 69 A.D. than did the general whom Nero sent to attack Jerusalem. Whether this eighth head was Otho, Vitellius, or Vespasian, however, there was no longer a true "Caesar." When Nero committed suicide, the last of the Caesarean dynasty died. Vespasian represented a new family on the throne—The Flavian dynasty. Nero was the Beast whose name meant "666." An Aramaic document of Nero's reign from the Wadi Murabba'at, in Jordan, contains the required spelling for Nero Caesar which would equal six hundred sixty-six in either Aramaic or Hebrew. (In Aramaic and Hebrew, letters stood for numbers—in a manner similar to the way Latin letters do in Roman numerals.) With the death of Nero, the entire Caesarean dynasty of emperors (the Beast) could be thrown into the Lake of Fire. The dynasty never returned. The other individual (besides the Beast) who was thrown into the Lake of Fire, at this point, was the "False Prophet" (Revelation 19:20). I explain in Chapter 4 of my book *Revelation: The Human Drama*, specifically with respect to "priestly" terminology, John's "false prophet" is probably a high priestly reference. John's description of the "second beast" is probably also a reference to the high priestly family. His "image of the beast" and the name "Babylon" are probably also high priestly references. With the destruction of Jerusalem, the entire (Babylonian) high priestly family that had usurped the high priesthood (with the help of Herod the Great) was destroyed—never again to preside over any sacrifices in the Temple (which was also destroyed).

With this destruction, the False Prophet/Babylon/image of the Beast could be thrown into the Lake of Fire. Revelation is true until proven false.

8. **The Dragon in the Abyss/Bottomless Pit.** In Revelation, the Dragon is progressively defeated. First, he (the Dragon) is cast out of heaven (Revelation 12:9-10). Apparently, this occurred when Jesus died and paid the price for the sins of humanity. There is, therefore, no longer any room for an "accuser" in heaven. Then, he is chained and confined in the Abyss for a thousand years (Revelation 20:1-3). Then, before the End, he will be released from the Abyss for some time for his last battle—of Gog and Magog (Revelation

20:3, 7-9). Finally, at the End, he is cast into the Lake of Fire (Revelation 20:10). The Abyss is not Hell. It is not a place that no one can ever escape from. Revelation 11:7 speaks of the Beast who comes up from the abyss "conquering" God's two witnesses--i.e., killing them. If he can come up from the Abyss, being confined to the Abyss is not a final judgment situation. It is only a temporary quieting of his activities. Which of his activities are quieted? "Deceiving the Nations" (Revelation 20:3 and 8).

9. **Thousand Year Reign.** Caird writes: "We return therefore to the question raised by the very first sentence of the Revelation. What did John think was 'bound to happen soon'? Certainly not the End, which was at least a millennium away." Which prophecies did John expect to happen near/short/quickly? The PAROUSIA? (Yes. See Chapter 14). The Fall of Jerusalem? Yes, it is a historical fact. History records it in almost as much gory detail as John prophesied. The beginning of the Thousand-year reign (The Millennium)? Yes. The destruction of the Beast and the False Prophet in the Lake of Fire? Yes. The imprisonment of the Dragon? Yes. The End of history? **No.** There is a cyclical plot in John's description of the reign of the Messiah. The messianic reign begins on the heels of the Battle (of Armageddon) in which a woman—the harlot Babylon—is destroyed (16:16ff.), and it ends with a Battle (of Gog and Magog) which a different woman—the "new Jerusalem"—wins. It begins with a preliminary defeat of the Dragon, with his being imprisoned in the abyss (20:3), and ends with the ultimate defeat of the Dragon, his being cast into the lake of fire (20:10). Having destroyed the harlot Babylon in the battle of Armageddon, the Lamb and his bride celebrate and rule the earth in 19.1-20.6. The beast

and the false prophet (Rome and the Jewish High Priesthood) are cast into the lake of fire. The Dragon/Satan is confined for a thousand years to the Abyss. The Christian martyrs are resurrected and reign for one thousand years with Christ. Since the significance of confining the Dragon to the Abyss was to curtail his activities of "deceiving the nations," it is interesting to note that (despite successive world empires—Babylonian, Mede-Persian, Greek, and Roman—for hundreds of years), with the Fall of the Roman Empire, world empires vanished for a thousand years. Calculate the thousand years from the death of Nero in 68 A.D. to 1068 A.D. or from the Christianizing of Rome under Constantine in 313 A.D. to 1313 A.D. Either way, you are brought to the Renaissance. For the thousand years prior to the Renaissance--as my professor of Ancient Greek Poetry at Indiana University, Willis Barnstone (nominated four times for the Pulitzer Prize in Poetry), first brought to my attention—Christian literature dominated the world and secular literature was progressively destroyed "FOR A THOUSAND YEARS." Furthermore, there was a thousand-year gap in the military atrocities of the great world empires. For example:

> During their first war with Carthage, a Roman fleet with 100,000 men was lost in a single day. Rome responded to this catastrophic loss by calmly sending in more troops and continuing the war for another *decade and a half.* Over the course of the second Carthaginian War, Rome suffered nearly 400,000 casualties without batting an eye. The Roman Empire wasn't really interested in outwitting its opponents -- it just outlasted them. If Rome had a problem, it kept throwing troops at it until it stopped causing trouble. When the Roman Empire fractured, Europe's economy became increasingly localized.   Without an intercontinental tax base and a healthy division of

labor, giant standing armies became artifacts of a bygone era. This sudden lack of fiscal infrastructure also left the scores of kings and princes who filled the Roman power vacuum strapped for cash. Sure, they probably would have *wanted* to roar through the continent with a million men, legion style; they just didn't have the money to pay such huge armies. Most leaders responded to this problem by introducing a feudal system; they divided and distributed their land holdings, dealing out plots for military service. Since very few of them had all that much land to begin with, this kept the armies relatively tiny -- even the most massive military forces of the latter stages of the era had well under 20,000 soldiers. Most armies were basically just large mobs. As such, warfare in the Dark Ages was defined by quick skirmishes fought between tiny forces. There were no campaigns, no decade-long struggles. (http://www.cracked.com/article_20615_5-ridiculous-myths-you-probably-believe-about-dark-ages.html)

And, what about Jesus and his martyrs reigning? To demonstrate the increasing reign of Jesus and his martyrs, it would be useful to show a picture of a world increasingly under the rule of the laws and teachings of Jesus. Such is the historical truth. Christianity has experienced astronomical growth, over the years. According to an even antagonistic source, http://commonsenseatheism.com/?p=95:

Christianity may have grown from about 1,000 believers in 40 C.E. to about 5-8 million in 300 C.E. – just 260 years. That would require a growth rate of **40% per decade**, as shown by this table:

Year	Number of Christians, given 40% growth per decade
40	1,000
50	1,400
60	1,960
70	2,744
80	3,842
90	5,378
100	7,530
150	40,496
200	217,795
250	1,171,356
300	6,299,832

. . . That really is tremendous growth."

According to http://mb-soft.com/believe/txx/numberch.htm:

Growth of the Church in Numbers:

Era	Estimated Christians
First century	500,000
Second century	2,000,000
Third century	5,000,000
Fourth century	10,000,000
Fifth century	15,000,000
Sixth century	20,000,000
Seventh century	24,000,000
Eighth century	30,000,000
Ninth century	40,000,000
Tenth century	50,000,000
Eleventh century	70,000,000
Twelfth century	80,000,000
Thirteenth century	75,000,000
Fourteenth century	80,000,000
Fifteenth century	100,000,000
Sixteenth century	125,000,000
Seventeenth century	155,000,000
Eighteenth century	200,000,000

A current pie chart of the world's religions, somewhat replicating the chart supplied by http://www.adherents.com/Religions_By_Adherents.html looks something like this one:

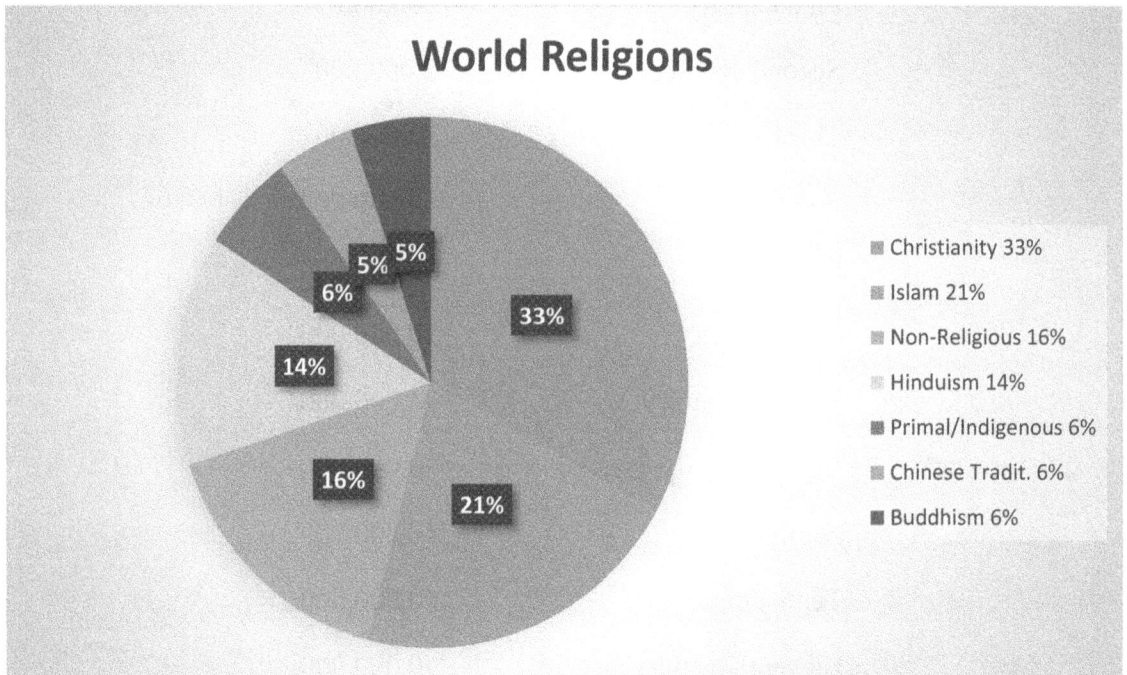

World Religions

- Christianity 33%
- Islam 21%
- Non-Religious 16%
- Hinduism 14%
- Primal/Indigenous 6%
- Chinese Tradit. 6%
- Buddhism 6%

I think that we can historically say that not only Revelation's prediction that Jesus' witnesses "lived and reigned with Christ a thousand years" (Revelation 20:4), but also that Revelation's prediction that the God and Christ "shall reign for ever and ever" (Revelation 11:15, 22:5) came true and is continuing to come true.

10. Satan's Release after the Thousand Years. Revelation 20:7-15 describes the final events of humanity's earthly existence. After the thousand years, Satan is released to raise one final army to fight against the camp of God's people, the city he loves. Once again, he "deceives the nations." In Chapter 3: The Four Logical Explosions of Human History," I pointed to the writings of the atheist John Thomas Didymus, and his article "Failed End-of-World Predictions of Jesus' Coming: Montanists and the Ecumenical Council (1000 A.D.)":

> The Ecumenical Council sitting in 999 declared solemnly that the world would end on January 1, 1000 A.D. That was the signal for mass madness. On the last day of the year, St. Peter's at Rome was filled with a crazed mass of people, weeping, trembling, screaming in fear of the Day of the Lord. They thought that God would send fire from heaven and burn the world to ashes . . . But New Year came and passes [sic] and nothing happened. (Article Source: http://EzineArticles.com/5476263).

I credited that 1000 A.D. event (or lack of an event) for shocking the world into the Renaissance (a logical abandonment of the teaching of the Church), because the Church had relied on the Book of Revelation (aka, the Apocalypse) in predicting that Jesus' reign on earth would last one thousand years. Certainly, the Ecumenical Council believed that John's Revelation was predicting that the BEGINNING of the thousand-year reign and the thousand-year imprisonment of the Dragon (aka, the Millennium) would be during the First Century A.D. The impetus for the Renaissance began when Christians' faith in the end of the world did not materialize at the time they expected it. Not only did the Renaissance bring with it a rebirth of humanism, but also a new rise in "nationalism." According to http://www.flowofhistory.com/units/west/11/FC79:

> Just as the turmoil of the Later Middle Ages had cleared the way for sweeping economic, cultural, and technological changes in Western

Europe, it likewise produced significant political changes that led to the emergence of a new type of state in Western Europe: the nation state.

Is it mere coincidence that Revelation predicted a millennium in which the Dragon (who raised up world powers) would be inhibited in his "deceiving the nations" only to be released at the end of the thousand years to "deceive the nations" again? Yet, this happened! As cited earlier, "Rome suffered nearly 400,000 casualties without batting an eye." By contrast, as noted earlier, during the millennium following the Roman Empire, "warfare . . . was defined by quick skirmishes fought between tiny forces. There were no campaigns, no decade-long struggles." But, once the thousand years were concluded, the deceiving of the "nations" begins again. From the Hundred Years War of the 14th and 15th centuries to the War of Roses to the Italian Wars to two World Wars of the 20th Century, clearly, nationalism and attempts at creating new world empires have been rising. Revelation's predictions are, once again, true. The Dragon has been released.

11. **The Battle of Gog and Magog.** So, now we look to the future predictions of Revelation. Satan's final world powers, Gog and Magog, are destroyed by fire. Who are these entities? We don't know, but we may speculate. What about Gog and Magog? What about the surrounding of the beloved city? Now, Hal Lindsey, you may try your hand. These were futuristic for John. The symbols used are much more ambiguous and, thus, open to speculation. Christians can surely supply interpretations that acknowledge the strength of the Contemporary-Historical method and yet preserve the expectant hope for the future triumphant return of Christ.

12. The End of Satan, Death, and the Old Earth. Satan and all whose names are not found in the book of life are thrown into the lake of fire. Death itself is thrown into the lake of fire. The epilogue, chapters 21 and 22, describe the new heavens and new earth in which the Lamb and his bride will spend eternity.

These final two prophecies have not, to the best of my knowledge, yet been fulfilled. But, what does that prove? It proves only that the world is continuing to exist. It does not prove that it will always continue. Revelation is true until proven false.

Chapter 16

The Gospels (and Acts) are True until Proven False

In May of 2013, I presented a scholarly paper at Ghent University, Belgium, in which I discussed the Beatitudes in Matthew and Luke and the nature of the Gospel genre. The title of my presentation was "Burke's Entelechy, Perelman's Epideictic, and the Transmission of Values." The conference was the **Rhetoric as Equipment for Living (Kenneth Burke, Culture, and Education) Conference**. It was the first European conference devoted to the study of the concepts of Kenneth Burke. While I consider Kenneth Burke to be the premier rhetorical theorist of the 20th Century, another close contender for that honor is Chaïm Perelman, who, during his lifetime, taught at the Free University of Brussels.

I was honored to have in the audience at my presentation not only elite Burkean scholars from across the globe, but also the Belgian scholar who had succeeded Perelman as Professor of

Rhetoric and Philosophy at the Free University of Brussels, Michel Meyer, a former student of Chaïm Perelman. During the Question-and-Answer period following my presentation, Professor Meyer took it upon himself to question the historicity of every one of the Gospels. He asserted that there was no difference between the Gospels and the story of Pinocchio. He asserted that anything that was written sixty years after the supposed historical event (which he asserted that the Gospels were) is nothing but fable. I continued the conversation with Professor Meyer, following the session at which I spoke, and subsequently published a journal article on the topic—at the urging of other Belgian scholars—in the *KB Journal* (Volume 11, Issue 1 Summer 2015), entitled "Burke, Perelman, and the Transmission of Values: The Beatitudes as Epideictic Topoi."

Professor Meyer's objection to the historicity of the Gospels is typical of many biblical scholars who, since the last third of the nineteenth century, have exchanged the previously overwhelming consensus that the Bible is the infallible Word of God for a new presumption—that the Scriptures are "a singular human book rather than a divine revelation" (Mark A. Noll, *Between Faith and Criticism*, 13). The Society of Biblical Literature (of which, incidentally, I am a member) was founded in 1880, and generally accepted assumptions, such as "that all religion reflects an evolutionary development from the primitive to the complex . . . and that supernatural events are not possible" (Noll, 20). Thus, a paradigm shift developed, between 1880 and 1900, for studying the Bible. The new paradigm dictated: "[T]he Bible . . . is a human book to be investigated with the standard assumptions that one brings to the discussion of all products of human culture" (Noll, 45).

Of course, that new liberal paradigm was a product of Modernism, which itself is now considered a failed philosophy. However, as it turns out, even according to that Modernist paradigm of studying the Bible as a "human book," the Gospels still shine as being historically reliable. Most liberal scholars now place the writing of the gospels within forty to sixty years after Jesus' earthly life. These critical scholars typically place the writing of Mark in the 70s A.D., Matthew and Luke in the 80s A.D., and John in the 90s A.D. If Jesus died in 33 A.D., and the earliest gospel was written in the 70s A.D., the gospel accounts began to be written down around forty years after Jesus' earthly life. However, it is by no means certain that the liberal scholarly dating of the gospels is correct. Dr. Craig Blomberg argues that the Book of Acts could not have been written later than 62 A.D., because it concludes with the Apostle Paul still living under house arrest in Rome, yet Paul was put to death sometime between 62 A.D. and 67 A.D. Since Acts was written by Luke AFTER Luke wrote his gospel, the Gospel According to Luke was probably written no later than 61 A.D. Since Luke appears to rely somewhat on Mark, Mark would apparently have been written no later than 60 A.D. If Jesus died in 33 A.D. and Mark was written as late as 60 A.D., the first gospel was written only 27 years after the events it describes. Is it possible for eyewitnesses to reconstruct historical events in detail correctly 30 or 40 or even 60 years after the fact? Absolutely!

I offer a personal example:

My brother Rod emailed a sister, another brother, and me, recently, recalling a car trip our family took 60 years ago. Rod wrote:

Barb your trip reminds me of the 1957 trip to Pikes Peak. Dad picked up the new '57 pea green Ford in Mason City. We stopped overnight at Uncle Ted's and they took us by Harry Truman's house. Then on to the Kansas sod house with Dennis in the cowboy outfit. Then it was the disappointment of the real Dodge City and Boot Hill. On toward Colorado with Marilyn saying, "Mom, make the boys sit still." Stan saying, "Are we there yet?" Tim saying, "Dad make Barb drive faster!" With Stan joining him in saying, "Yeah, let's go 80."

In the spirit of eyewitness confirmation, Barb wrote back: "Wow Rod what a memory! . . . It seemed like many times Dad packed us all into the car in the early morning to make a trip --always so pleasant to be riding as the sun came up." To illustrate the corrective nature of eyewitnesses, I then responded:

Rod is mistaken about me saying, "Let's go 80." I recall that the line came from one of the children Uncle Emery used to take to church. The child told him, "Let's go faster, Henry! Let's go 50." The story was related to me by Sam. I do remember how exciting it was to be surprised at school by having Dad pick us up in a new car and take off on vacation.

Rod, then, corroborated my account of the "let's go faster" line:

Cindy Hartey implored "Henry" to go faster, and her brother said, "Yeah, Henry, let's go 50," when our super uncle was already going 60. Taking that lead, Barb's brothers implored her to drive faster and upped the ante to "Let's go 80." I was with Dad when he picked up that '57 Ford. He loved the collar [Dad's pronunciation of the word: color] he chose and ordered. He was so disappointed when it over-heated, so we didn't reach the top of the mountain. But it was only a six cylinder and was loaded to the hilt with him, Mom, six kids and a trunk crammed with luggage. I loved his driving on those terribly narrow mountain roads. His wheels were often too close to the edge for Mom's sanity. And he had to back up to a wider place in the road several times upon meeting other cars. On the way to CO it was really good of him to give our 17-year-old sister a chance to drive. On the way home, I think he must have been pretty tired of driving and, if Barb would drive, he would not back-seat-drive and have her go 80 NO MATTER HOW MUCH YOU AND TIM YELLED AT HER!!!!! But, Stan, you will be most pleased to learn that for the first time in family history Mom, Barb, and Marilyn ordered this new food called pizza in Colorado Springs, the night before we attempted the trip up the mountain. Of course, we boys didn't even try it because we thought it had to be yuk.

I deferred to my older brother's recollection but added a caveat:

You are correct. It was Cindy (although, for some reason, I had envisioned her last name as being spelled "Hardy") and the joke was that Uncle Emery had already been going 60, at the time. I suppose that it is possible that I upped the ante to 80 on that trip--I would have only been 7 years old at the time. What I find fascinating about these interactions regarding our past shared history is the way they corroborate the "historical" facticity of the Gospel accounts. . . . It emphasizes to me that these events happened 60 years ago, yet we eyewitnesses are able to supply recalcitrance (both corrective and corroborative) to reconstruct even the minute details of conversations and events that occurred so long ago. If we "kids" can do this sort of thing sixty years after the events, it would be a piece of cake for Jesus' hundreds and thousands of eyewitness disciples to supply this kind of recalcitrance regarding the sermons, teachings, conversations, and events of Jesus' life that were recorded by Paul (just a few years after Jesus' death and resurrection in I Corinthians 15:1-9, where he mentions hundreds of eyewitnesses) or his student and assistant Dr. Luke or Peter's student Mark or the actual eyewitnesses Matthew and John, within only 40 years after the events. And our reconstructions are accomplished even without the considerable benefit of the spiritual gifts of Apostles and Evangelists! . . . Dennis--being a later arrival, like the Apostle Paul--gets to confer with us original experiencers to discover the details he was not around to experience. However, when Barb shoots us those pictures of her and Marilyn and the Flood, I find myself in Dennis and Paul's situation, as well!

Rod, then modified his account of me saying "Let's go eighty":

I confess, you may not have egged Barb to drive faster. It was Tim and I who coined the word squeighty on that trip. I cannot imagine why a 17-year-old girl wouldn't feel safe driving 80 on a two-lane road with her family of [eight] shoehorned into a little '57 Ford. My memory and faith (even in Barb's driving) fail miserably when compared to Matthew's and John's ability to recount events and statements. Methinks, it is the difference between blowing smoke and the Holy Spirit giving utterance. I debated Hardy and Hartey and thought it was the latter.

Finally, Dennis, who was just a baby at the time of the trip we discussed, joined in to confirm the Cindy Hardy story, but in a somewhat tongue-in-cheek manner, threw in the concept of textual variants:

I also remember the Cyndi Hardee story (note the textual variant!), though, obviously not from personal eyewitness experience. Stan, your implied designation of me as "one untimely born" makes a lot of sense and helps me with my own self-understanding a bit. Being untimely born has its pros and cons. On the one hand, . . . I have little to no personal connection with our Lindsay cousins – certainly not the way you elderly siblings have. On the other hand, it affords me a unique perspective/voice in the family, not necessarily anchored to some of the earlier family experiences and experiments.

Having some fun with Dennis's allusion to the similarities between the Apostle Paul and himself, I replied: "Right, Dennis! Don't push the metaphor too far! :) Were you thinking of making Rod into Cephas and Barb into the Magdalene? I, being somewhat younger than Rod, am content with being the disciple whom Jesus loved."

If this exchange among my family members seems excessively conscious of critical Biblical issues, it is because my brother Dennis holds a Doctor of Theology degree from the University of Tübingen and both my brother Rod and Barb's husband, Dean, are Christian ministers, both holding the M.Div. degree from Lincoln Christian University. Yet, I repeat my observation:

> What I find fascinating about these interactions regarding our past shared history is the way they corroborate the "historical" facticity of the Gospel accounts. . . . It emphasizes to me that these events happened 60 years ago, yet we eyewitnesses are able to . . . reconstruct even the minute details of conversations and events that occurred so long ago. If we [OLD] "kids" can do this sort of thing sixty years after the events, it would be a piece of cake for Jesus' hundreds and thousands of

eyewitness disciples to supply this kind of recalcitrance regarding the sermons, teachings, conversations, and events of Jesus' life . . . within only 40 years after the events.

And, this example of our reconstruction of events in our childhood is typical. We have done this type of reconstruction countless times, regarding countless shared events in our lives. I'm sure that we are not alone. Virtually everyone could verify this type of phenomenon occurring in his/her life.

Crowdsourcing, a term coined in 2005, conceptualizes some of the very phenomena that I have just described from familial and Gospel contexts. The primary difference is that the internet is now used to cross-check and verify information, whether used for ideas, services, marketing, or even Wikipedia, which offers the following definition: "Crowdsourcing is distinguished from outsourcing in that the work can come from an undefined public (instead of being commissioned from a specific, named group) and in that crowdsourcing includes a mix of bottom-up and top-down processes." On October 2, 2017, I watched the premier episode of a television show, "Wisdom of the Crowd," which shows the crowdsourcing methodology being used to solve crimes. This is similar to what occurred as the Gospels were being formulated.

The Gospels, however, were not the first written accounts of events in the life of Jesus. The earliest written record of events in the life of Jesus occurs, not in the Gospels, but in the epistles of Paul, written in the 40s and 50s. Professor Meyer's assertion that anything that was written sixty years after the supposed historical event (which he asserted that the Gospels were) is nothing but fable begins to unravel with the fact that Paul, in I Corinthians 15:3-8 (KJV), gives an outline of the most important section of the Gospels (occurring in all 4 gospels and Acts):

> [3] For what I received I passed on to you as of first importance: that Christ died for our sins according to the Scriptures, [4] that he was buried, that he was raised on the third day according to the Scriptures, [5] and that he appeared to Cephas, and then to the Twelve. [6] After that, he appeared to more than five hundred of the brothers and sisters at the same time, most of whom are still living, though some have fallen asleep. [7] Then he appeared to James, then to all the apostles, [8] and last of all he appeared to me also, as to one abnormally born.

WHEN did Paul receive this account of Jesus' death, burial, and resurrection on the third day, plus his appearances to his disciples (the related events of which take up one-half of the Gospel according to Mark)? He certainly received it BEFORE he wrote the book of I Corinthians. The most logical suggestion is that he received the account sometime in the three years following his conversion on the Road to Damascus, at which time Paul himself became an eyewitness of the resurrected Jesus. That event occurred approximately two years after Jesus' death, and Paul (previously called Saul of Tarsus) had surely heard some of the gospel message, beforehand, because he had been actively persecuting the Christian sect for their message. He would have known some of the claims of the sect he was persecuting. Within three years of his conversion, he learned the gospel more fully from Ananias in Damascus and, eventually, three years later, from Peter and James (Jesus' brother) in Jerusalem: "After three years I went up to Jerusalem to visit Cephas and remained with him fifteen days. But I saw none of the other apostles except James the

Lord's brother" (Galatians 1:18-19). If Paul is passing along information that he received within the first five years after Jesus' earthly life, Professor Meyer's assertion that these biblical accounts are non-historical because they are all written too many years after the fact is unraveling even FASTER. Paul's writings confirm the Gospel accounts that:

1.   Jesus was a direct descendent of King David (Romans 1:3, II Timothy 2:8)

2.   Jesus' brother was James--the son of Joseph and Mary (I Corinthians 15:3-8, Galatians 1:19, 2:9, 12)

3.   Jesus had twelve disciples (I Corinthians 15:3-8)

4.   Jesus is the Christ, the Jewish Messiah, the Son of God (throughout Paul's writings)

5.   Miracles truly do occur (I Corinthians 12:10, 28-29)

6.   Healings truly do occur (I Corinthians 12:9, 28, 30)

7.   Jesus was transfigured (Philippians 2:5-11)

8.   Jesus introduced the Lord's Supper (I Corinthians 11:23-26)

9.   Jesus was betrayed (I Corinthians 11:23)

10.   Jesus was killed by the method of crucifixion (Philippians 2:5-11)

11.   Jesus truly died (I Corinthians 15:3-8, Philippians 2:5-11)

12.   Jesus was buried (I Corinthians 15:4, Romans 6:4, Colossians 2:12)

13. Jesus was resurrected in three days (I Corinthians 15:4, II Timothy 2:8)

14. Jesus appeared in resurrected form to Peter and the twelve (I Corinthians 15:3-8)

15. Jesus appeared in resurrected form to many others (I Corinthians 15:3-8)

16. Jesus was exalted in heaven (Philippians 2:5-11)

17. Jesus promised to return soon, in his PAROUSIA (I Corinthians 15:23 and 51-52).

If liberal scholars generally accept assumptions such as "that supernatural events are not possible" (Noll, 20), they would tend to write off all miracles and healings in the Gospel accounts. I wrote, in Chapter 15:

As I point out in my book *ArguMentor*,

> Miracles and fulfilled prophecies are proofs that do not necessarily rely on *ethos* [and, hence, are logical, relying on *logos*]. However, ACCOUNTS of miracles, absent substantiating evidence, do again rely on *ethos*. It is generally advisable in argumentation not to rely excessively on *ethos*, unless both parties in the dispute are willing to stipulate that the individual (or individuals) being relied on for *ethos* is in a position to know the truth of a matter.'

. . . How would one ever prove that Jesus was born of a virgin, or that he walked on water, changed water into wine, fed 5000 with two fish and five loaves of bread, raised Lazarus from the dead, and performed numerous healings? Conversely, how would one ever disprove those things? One just has to TRUST the person/s relating the account. Of course, in the case of the gospel accounts of miracles, apostles and eyewitnesses were willing to die instead of recanting their testimonies.

The writings of Josephus and other Jewish writers from the period do nothing to disclaim accounts of Jesus' miraculous works, although the Talmud credits "sorcery" as the basis upon which he accomplished the works.

Logically, it seems to me the height of arrogance to suggest that feats that defy nature that have been accomplished by other human beings would be IMPOSSIBLE to accomplish by someone who received power from God. **Except, possibly, for "raising the dead (after they had been dead for 3 days)," virtually every type of healing the Gospels attribute to Jesus has been accomplished, over the years, by medical science.** Chapter 3 of my book *Implicit Rhetoric: Kenneth Burke's Extension of Aristotle's Concept of Entelechy* is entitled "The Human as Super-*Natural*: Aristotelian Types of Entelechy." The premise of the chapter is a clause from Kenneth Burke's Definition of Human. The clause is that the human is "separated from his[/her] **natural** condition by instruments of his[/her] own making" (LSA 16, bold mine). If even we humble mortals have the capacity to overcome natural laws and conditions, how arrogant must we be to insist that God's Son would never be able to defy natural laws?

The following list of illnesses and bodily malfunctions cured by Jesus is fairly complete:

- Bent spine—Luke 13:10-21 (crippled woman)

- Blind—John 9:1-41 (man born that way); Mark 10:46-52; Matthew 20: 29-34; Luke 18:35-43; Matthew 11:2-19; Luke 7:18-35

- Deaf—Matthew 11:2-19; Luke 7:18-35

- Diseases—Matthew 11:2-19; Luke 7:18-35

- Epileptic—Matthew 4:23-25

- Fever—John 4:46-54; Mark 1:29-34; Matthew 8:14-17; Luke 4:38-41

- Lame—John 1:5-47; Matthew 11:2-19; Luke 7:18-35

- Leprosy—Luke 17:11-37; Mark 1:40-45; Matthew 8:2-4; Luke 5:12-16; Matthew 11:2-19; Luke 7:18-35

- Palsy—Mark 2:1-12; Matthew 9:1-8; Luke 5:17-26 (paralytic?); Matthew 4:23-25; Matthew 8:5-13; Luke 7:1-10 (near death)

- Plagues—Matthew 11:2-19; Luke 7:18-35

- Sick on their beds—Mark 6:53-56; Matthew 14;34-36

- Various illnesses—Mark 1:29-34; Matthew 8:14-17; Luke 4:38-41

- Withered hand—Mark 3:1-6; Matthew 12:9-14; Luke 6:6-11

- Raise dead—Matthew 11:2-19; Luke 7:18-35; John 11:1-44 (Lazarus); Luke 7:11-17

Of course, being born of a virgin, walking on water, changing water into wine, feeding five thousand with two fish and five loaves of bread, and raising Lazarus from the dead are qualitatively much more substantial miracles than most of the healings Jesus effected. But what greater miracle was there in all of history than Jesus' resurrection from death by crucifixion? And, Paul's early testimony of more than five hundred eyewitnesses of Jesus' resurrection argues strongly that the Gospel accounts were confirmed by the testimony of hundreds of eyewitnesses.

In Lee Strobel's powerful book, *The Case for Christ*, he interviews thirteen scholars with excellent credentials for attesting to the historical reliability of the Gospels. I recommend that readers purchase the audiobook version of this text and listen to it again and again. Strobel is a former legal editor of the *Chicago Tribune*. He approaches the issue of whether Christianity is reliable from a legal/forensic perspective, as he calls scholarly witnesses. His chapters focus on issues such as whether the eyewitness testimony in the Gospels is credible, whether the text of the Gospels have been reliably transmitted through the years, whether there is corroborating testimony concerning the historical reliability of the Gospels from other historical sources, whether archaeology confirms details found in the Gospels, etc. Strobel's interviews supply answers for a multitude of attacks that have been made against the Gospels.

Certainly, as Strobel himself admits in a subsequent interview, it would be impossible to offer answers for every attack that has been launched against the Gospels in a single book. Yet, many of the most important attacks are considered. One such attack that is not covered by Strobel is one that I personally had the most difficulty with while studying in the Graduate School at Indiana University. One incidental verse in the text of John 19 was nearly fatal to my faith, as I studied for my Master's in Hebrew at Indiana University, back in the 1970s. At Indiana, I had studied at the feet of scholars who were not only Biblical scholars, but also, *especially*, Jewish scholars, who had absolutely no vested interest in helping me defend the Christian scriptures. I came home to my wife, Linda, on many occasions, saying that Biblical problems had been presented to me for which I had no answers. Linda always said, "Just keep your faith; there will be answers."

But one day, I came home from class and said, "I think they have finally done it. They have shown me an error in the New Testament for which there can be no answer." The Jewish scholar who pointed it out even stated that, while Christian apologists have found answers to other Biblical problems, this is the one obvious contradiction that no one has ever been able to solve: The synoptic gospels claim that the disciples ate the Passover Meal with his disciples before he was crucified. You can't take an "absentee" Passover Meal like you vote with an "absentee" ballot. No one eats the Passover until the evening of the first night (Friday night, being the beginning of Sabbath) of the Passover Week. The paschal lamb is killed in the afternoon, before that meal. But, according to John (19:14, et. al.), Jesus was crucified at the same time they killed the lamb (on the day of Preparation). He was dead and in the tomb at the time when the Passover was eaten. This was presented to me as the ultimate proof that the Gospels made an error. Romans 3:4 (KJV) says, "God must be true though every man be a liar," and in John 10:35 (KJV), Jesus says, "Scripture cannot be broken." Still, I trusted my wife's admonition.

Just TWO days later, I was reading one of Millar Burrows's books on the Dead Sea Scrolls, and it jumped out at me. It virtually slapped my face and said, "Don't ever doubt Me again (just as Jesus implicitly scolded Thomas for doubting)!" I suspect that there was some Providence involved. It seems that among the Dead Sea Scrolls, a calendar was found that disagreed with the official calendar of the Jerusalem temple cult. The Essenes (from whom John the Baptist and his disciples came, some of whom subsequently became Jesus' disciples) followed a different calendar with a different date for Passover (and the day of Preparation). There were at least two different dates for the first day of Passover in Jesus' time. It was possible for the synoptic gospels to have used a different calendar when they said that Jesus ate the Passover meal before he died. They say that whatever doesn't kill you makes you stronger. I learned. My faith has been thoroughly intact since then.

Christians will certainly come across issues that non-Christians argue should be obstacles to believing in the truth and infallibility of the scriptures. Virtually everything a Christian might face has someone (usually cited on the internet) who offers plausible answers for the issue. We return to Professor Meyer's teacher, Chaïm Perelman. As I stated, Perelman states on pages 24-25 of the *Realm of Rhetoric* that presumption "imposes the burden of proof upon the person who wants to oppose its application." These are some of my presumptions:

- The resurrection did occur.

- God did create the universe.

- The Bible is inspired of God.

Furthermore, these are presumptions held by a massive Christian Culture. My presumption is that these premises are "true, until proven false." If others want to prove that the Bible is false, they must first determine every possible meaning of every Greek, Hebrew, and Aramaic word in the Scriptures. Then, they must consider every conceivable grammatical combination in which those words may be found. Next, they must consider every possible trope, every figure of speech, as a means of determining the multitudinous possible interpretations of every verse of scripture. And, they must disprove not just one or two interpretations that they might prefer to debunk, in a "straw man" logical fallacy approach. They must disprove every single interpretation that is remotely possible—that has been previously advanced or that will be advanced at any point in the future. The Gospels are true, until proven false.

Chapter 17

And, Batting Cleanup: The Holy Spirit

The link in the syllogistic chain I presented in the previous chapter pertains to the argument that, even if the Bible were considered a thoroughly human book—written by humans without divine aid and collected and canonized by humans without divine aid—still (logically) the Bible is trustworthy. But, why do we tie our hands behind our back? Why would logical individuals restrict their arguments to some such arbitrary presumption—simply because scholars operating under a now-defunct, now-bankrupt modernist philosophy that demanded that we doubt everything that can be doubted prescribed such a presumption?

On pages 41-42, I argue:

> It is altogether CONSISTENT that LOGOS THE AGENT used LOGOS THE
> AGENCY to self-actualize in the ACT of creating a LOGICAL UNIVERSE
> capable of sustaining LIFE and, consequently, leading to a SCENE in which

SOCIAL PURPOSE motivated the AGENT to create a CREATIVE, COMMUNICATIVE, ACTION-BASED life form with which LOGOS THE AGENT could communicate.

I continue my argument on pages 44-45:

> It seems that, since the God we seek to identify uses "rational communication" for the purpose of developing "social" relationships with the only species to whom that God has given the ability to engage in creative "action"—namely, the human—the God we seek to identify should have, at least at some point, "communicated socially" with this human species. … Logically, a God capable of and motivated to communicate socially with a species that that God designed and formed to be capable of similar communicative action would be expected to engage in such social communication.

How does the Judeo-Christian God communicate with humans? I answer on page 67:

> The only ways that God still spoke freshly to humans, for Rabbinic Judaism, were through children, fools, and the BAT QOL (or mysterious voice from Heaven). Jesus alludes to the proofs of God speaking through children during his Palm Sunday entry into Jerusalem (Matthew 21:15-16). And, while Christianity disagrees [with the Jewish view] that the age of prophecy had ended (there are plenty of Christian prophecies), it certainly affords the proof that was still acceptable to Jews: The BAT QOL.

On page 82, I add:

> It seems that both children and fools were considered innocent, because they lack the good inclination. Therefore, the Holy Spirit (which inspires prophecy) is able to dwell inside these humans—they are innocent—in the same logical move that prompted Acts 2:17-18 to report that (after Jesus' death and resurrection) "the Spirit" could be "poured out" on all flesh. Once Jesus' death provided the forgiveness, the "NOW innocent" believers could receive the Holy Spirit.

In Chapter 23 of my book *Angels and demons: The personification of communication*, I explain:

> Jewish scholar G. F. Moore (in Volume I, page 414, of his book *Judaism in the First Centuries of the Christian Era*) links . . . three terms . . . together quite easily. In his chapter entitled, "The Word of God: The Spirit," Moore states, "God's will is made known or effectuated in the world not only through personal agents (*ANGELS*), but directly by his *WORD* or by his *SPIRIT*" (emphases mine).

According to the Bible, God has spoken to humans through his own voice, his own handwriting, the BAT QOL, angels, and the Holy Spirit/Spirit of God. Many of such messages are recorded in the Bible. The Holy Spirit, according to Judaism, was—in times past—found in prophets, children, and fools. After Jesus' death and resurrection, the Holy Spirit could be "poured out" on all "flesh" (KJV). This is predicated on a prophecy given through the Old Testament prophet Joel—Joel 2:28: "And afterward, I will pour out my Spirit on all flesh/people. Your sons and daughters will prophesy, your old men will dream dreams, your young men will see visions." Acts 2:16-18 (NIV) in the New Testament, claims that the prophecy was fulfilled on the day of Pentecost (fifty days

after the death and resurrection of Jesus):

> [16] [T]his is what was spoken by the prophet Joel: [17] "In the last days," God says, "I
> will pour out my Spirit on all flesh/people. Your sons and daughters will prophesy,
> your young men will see visions, your old men will dream dreams. [18] Even on my
> servants, both men and women, I will pour out my Spirit in those days, and they
> will prophesy."

But was it literally poured out on ALL flesh? Not if, by all flesh, we mean animal flesh. (Hence,

the NIV translated "flesh" (the literal translation of both the Greek [SARX] and Hebrew

[BASHAR] terms) as "people." Not if, by all flesh, we mean all "people"—including non-

Christian humans. Not even if, by all flesh, we mean that every Christian is able to prophecy. Paul

asks rhetorically, in I Corinthians 12:29-30 (ASV): "Are all apostles? Are all prophets?" The

clearly implied (rhetorical question) answer is "No." Not even can it be said that every Christian

in New Testament times possessed a spiritual gift that would allow him or her to be a medium of

God's messages. Rather, these miraculous spiritual gifts are given by the "laying on of the hands

of apostles." In my book *Psychotic Entelechy: The Dangers of Spiritual Gifts Theology*, I observe:

> Christianity . . . believes that God continued to speak through the visitation of
> angels (as when Gabriel announced John's and Jesus' births) and through prophets
> and prophetesses such as Simeon and Anna (Luke 2:25-38) and especially through
> John the Baptist who lived at the time of Jesus. Christianity also teaches that God

spoke through those (such as apostles and prophets) who had received spiritual gifts in the first generation of the church.

According to *Catholic.com*:

> Catholics hold that public or "general" revelation ended at the death of the last apostle (*Catechism of the Catholic Church* 66, 73), but private revelations can be given still—and have been, as Marian apparitions at such places as Fatima and Lourdes testify (*CCC* 67). Such revelations can never correct, supplement, or complete the Christian faith ("Distinctive Beliefs of the Mormon Church," *Catholic Answers*. Available:

> http://www.catholic.com/library/Distinctive_Beliefs_of_Mormon.asp (10/15/05).

Protestantism as defined by Martin Luther claimed that God's communication with humans ended with the canonical Old and New Testaments. Luther's mantra, "Sola Scriptura," emphasized the point that even the Catholic Church in its various offices were not considered capable of credibly offering new messages from God (pp. 98-99).

I continue, in *Psychotic Entelechy: The Dangers of Spiritual Gifts Theology*, pages 110-112:

> Those who are "filled with the Spirit" are at [the] time [of the New Testament—the time that the Book of Acts refers to them] actually in the process of *receiving* messages from God. In addition to using the mediation of angels and mysterious voices, God (in the New Testament period) used a variety of methods to

communicate with humans. These methods are termed "spiritual gifts" by the apostle Paul. Yet, each method or gift was designed to provide communication from God.

The spiritual gifts listed by the apostle Paul in three separate writings feature prophets prominently (Romans 12:6, I Corinthians 12:28, Ephesians 4:11). In the last two lists, prophets are listed second only to apostles. In the first list, apostles are not mentioned; prophets are listed first. Both apostles and prophets had miraculous powers. Their messages, whether written or spoken, were considered by the Church to have come from God just as surely as the messages of Moses, Elijah, and David did. The early Christians met weekly to devote themselves not to the Torah (as the Jews did in the Synagogue), but to the apostles' doctrine (Acts 2:42). Of the twenty-seven books in the New Testament canon, at least seventeen were thought to have been authored by apostles. The Book of Revelation was written by a prophet. Luke and Acts were both written by the evangelist Luke, and Mark is attributed to the evangelist John Mark. In the Ephesians 4:11 list, evangelists are mentioned as (spiritually) gifted, immediately following apostles and prophets.

Hebrews and the three epistles of John were at one time thought to have been authored by the apostles Paul and John, respectively. None of the four epistles make the claim of apostolic authorship, however. Second and Third John claim to be written by "The Elder." If he is not the apostle John himself, the Elder is probably a prominent disciple of the apostle John. Given its Pauline elements, Hebrews may well have been written by a prominent disciple of the apostle Paul. James and Jude claim to have been written by Jesus' physical relatives: his brothers. All of the authors of New Testament books not authored by apostles or prophets could easily be authored by individuals who had other spiritual gifts. Paul seems to assert that he conveyed a spiritual gift of prophecy to Timothy at the time he laid hands on him to set him apart for eldership (I Timothy 4:14 and II Timothy 1:6). It is possible that the Elder of the epistles of John (if not the apostle John) also received a spiritual gift at his ordination as elder. The author of Hebrews claims to be a companion of Timothy (Hebrews 13:23). Hence, some think Paul is the author. If the author is not Paul, he may have received a spiritual gift from Paul as Timothy did. Jesus' brother James is depicted in Acts 15 as the presider among the apostles in Jerusalem. Paul lists James along with Peter and John as the pillars of the Jerusalem church (Galatians 2:9). Apparently, James had some form of inspiration, as his brother Jude may have.

The basis upon which Christians believe the books of the New Testament were inspired of God is that all books were written by authors who had spiritual gifts. Various lists of spiritual gifts mentioned in the New Testament include:

- apostles (I Corinthians 12:28-29, Ephesians 14:11),

- prophets (Romans 12:6, I Corinthians 12:10, 28-29, 14:1-40, Ephesians 14:11),

- evangelists (Ephesians 14:11),

- teachers (I Corinthians 12:28-29, 14:6, Ephesians 14:11),

- healers (I Corinthians 12:9, 28-29),

- miracle workers (I Corinthians 12:10, 28-29),

- pastors (Ephesians 14:11),

- deacons/servants (Romans 12:7),

- encouragers (Romans 12:8),

- contributors to the needs of others (Romans 12:8),

- leaders (Romans 12:8),

- mercy givers (Romans 12:8),

- helpers of others (I Corinthians 12:28),

- administrators (I Corinthians 12:28),

- revealer (I Corinthians 14:6)

- messengers of wisdom (I Corinthians 12:8),

- messengers of knowledge (I Corinthians 12:8, 14:6),

- believers--with the gift of faith (I Corinthians 12:9)

- speakers in tongues (I Corinthians 12:10, 28-30, 14:1-40), and

- interpreters of tongues (I Corinthians 12:10, 30).

Also listed by Paul among the spiritual gifts in Romans 12:7, some of the early deacons on whom the apostles laid hands were apparently prophets, healers, and miracle workers, as well (Acts 7:56, 8:5-7, 13). Some of the abilities listed as spiritual gifts could be interpreted as the equivalent of typical aptitudes without respect to any miraculous abilities. Many teachers, pastors, servants, encouragers, contributors, leaders, mercy givers, helpers, administrators, and believers have existed throughout the history of mankind without respect to any specific spiritual giftedness. But, then, what would be the point of calling them spiritual gifts? The miraculous element is implicit in the way Paul discusses spiritual gifts.

Incidentally, the receiving of spiritual gifts is not identical with what Acts describes as "baptism of the Holy Spirit"—an event that occurred on only two occasions. For a discussion of that phenomenon, which was accomplished by a separate act of God, consult my book *Psychotic Entelechy: The Dangers of Spiritual Gifts Theology*, pages 117-118. But, how were spiritual gifts conferred? I answer the question on pages 113-116:

> If spiritual gifts provide miraculous messages from God, it is important to know how they are conferred.
>
> . . .
>
> [T]he phenomenon referred to by the apostle Paul as "spiritual gifts" may be referred to by other New Testament writers with different terminology. While never using the phrase "spiritual gifts," Luke points out in Acts: "The apostles performed many miraculous signs and wonders among the people. . . . Crowds gathered . . . bringing their sick and those tormented by evil spirits, and all of them were healed" (Acts 5:12, 16).

The Laying On of Apostles' Hands

In the early period of the church, seven deacons were chosen to assist the apostles. Luke states: "They presented these men to the apostles, who prayed and laid their hands on them" (Acts 6:6). Afterwards, one of those deacons, "Stephen . . . did great wonders and miraculous signs among the people" (Acts 6:8). Another of the deacons, "Philip went down to a city in Samaria . . . the crowds heard Philip and saw the miraculous signs he did . . .   [E]vil spirits came out of many, and many paralytics and cripples were healed" (Acts 8:5-7). Although Luke never refers to these special abilities of the apostles and deacons as "spiritual gifts," their abilities seem to be identical to the abilities of the healers and miracle workers in Paul's lists of spiritual gifts.

Although Philip baptized many Samaritans, Philip was the only Christian in Samaria capable of performing miraculous works. Luke states: "[T]he Holy Spirit had not yet come upon any of them; they had simply been baptized into the name of the Lord Jesus. Then Peter and John placed their hands on them, and they received the Holy Spirit" (Acts 8:16-17). One must assume that receiving the Holy Spirit in Luke's terminology means that the Samaritan Christians were capable of miraculous works, as was Philip. A sorcerer named Simon noticed the method by which these gifts were transferred: "When Simon saw that the Spirit was given at the laying on of the apostles' hands, he offered them money and said, 'Give me also this ability so that everyone on whom I lay my hands may receive the Holy Spirit'" (Acts 8:18-19). His request was denied.

The laying on of the hands of an apostle seems to be the method by which spiritual gifts were conferred in the apostle Paul's writings. In Romans 1:11, Paul tells the Romans: "I long to see you so that I may impart to you some spiritual gift." Why was it necessary for the apostle to see the Romans in order to confer spiritual gifts? Could he not just pray that they would receive spiritual gifts? Apparently not. Did they not automatically receive spiritual gifts upon being baptized? The Samaritans who were baptized by the deacon Philip did not receive spiritual gifts at baptism. The Roman church was in a unique position. Apparently, some Roman Christians *did* have spiritual gifts or Paul would not have written in the twelfth chapter of his epistle:

> We have different gifts, according to the grace given us. If a man's gift is prophesying, let him use it in proportion to his faith. If it is serving, let him serve; if it is teaching, let him teach; if it is encouraging, let him encourage; if it is contributing to the needs of others, let him give generously; if it is leadership, let him govern

diligently; if it is showing mercy, let him do it cheerfully. (Romans 12:6-8)

Luke informs us that Jews and proselytes from Rome were in Jerusalem on the day of Pentecost (Acts 2:10-11). Some of these Romans were surely converted to Christianity by the apostles on that day. It is fair to assume that some of them received the laying on of the hands of apostles.

In Acts 19, Luke records another incident in which an apostle laid hands on some individuals and they received spiritual gifts. Paul discovered at Ephesus some disciples who had received only the baptism of repentance taught by John the Baptist, not Christian baptism. They were unaware of any Holy Spirit connection. Paul had them rebaptized in the name of Jesus. After the baptism, Luke reports: "When Paul laid his hands on them, the Holy Spirit came on them, and they spoke in tongues and prophesied" (Acts 19:6). Observing Luke's symbol system, the terminology he used in Acts 19--"receiving the Holy Spirit" and "the Holy Spirit coming on" individuals—is identical to the terminology he used in Acts 8:16-17, at which time the apostles Peter and John laid their hands on the first Samaritan Christians after their baptism. In the Acts 8 text, Simon the Sorcerer observed that (miraculous) gifts were given by the laying on of apostles' hands (Acts 8:18). Speaking in tongues is not clearly defined in the Acts 19 instance. Perhaps, it was the spiritual gift of prophecy discussed by Paul in I Corinthians 12-14. Prophecy, which is also mentioned as a result of the laying on of Paul's hands in Acts 19, is definitely a spiritual gift.

Paul informs Timothy that Timothy's spiritual gift was conferred when Paul laid hands on him: "For this reason I remind you to fan into flame the gift of God, which is in you through the laying on of my hands" (II Timothy 1:6). Some have suggested, based on I Timothy 4:14, that spiritual gifts were conferred by the laying on of the hands of non-apostles. Paul tells Timothy: "Do not neglect your gift, which was given to you through prophecy by the laying on of the hands of eldership." The proposed interpretation suggests that the gift was conferred when the body of elders laid their hands on Timothy. While that interpretation of the text is possible, it is also possible that the text should be interpreted: The prophetic gift was conferred on Timothy when Timothy was set apart as an elder through the laying on of hands. II Timothy 1:6 argues strongly for this second interpretation. Paul clearly tells Timothy his gift was conferred when Paul laid hands on him.

If we accept this second interpretation, we do not have a single instance in the entire New Testament of someone receiving a "spiritual gift" except by the laying on of an apostle's hands. This observation, of course, does not apply to the conferral of the gift of apostleship.

So, then, if spiritual gifts are only conferred by the laying on of an apostle's hands, how does one become an apostle? I answer on pages 119-120:

Requirements for Becoming an Apostle

According to the Revelation to John, Jesus praises the church at Ephesus for testing "those who claim to be apostles but are not" (Revelation 2:2). Revelation, however, does not spell out how false apostles are detected. Luke's writings identified . . . the method by which spiritual gifts were conferred—by the laying on of apostles' hands. It is suitable, then, that we turn to Luke for information regarding how men became apostles.

In Acts 1:12-2:4 . . . Luke details the choosing of a new apostle to take the place of Judas Iscariot. He quotes Peter in listing the qualifications for the office:

> Therefore, it is necessary to choose one of the men who have been
> with us the whole time the Lord Jesus went in and out among us,
> beginning from John's baptism to the time when Jesus was taken up
> from us. For one of these must be a witness with us of his
> resurrection. (Acts 1:21-22)

If, in order to be counted an apostle, one must have been a personal disciple of Jesus for at least three years and an eye witness of his resurrected body, it seems impossible that a modern-day apostle could exist. Even Paul apparently had those who questioned his apostleship. Clearly, Paul was not a personal disciple of Jesus during his ministry from John's baptism to Jesus' ascension. He could, however, on the basis of his conversion experience on the road to Damascus, claim to be a witness of the resurrected Jesus. He asks rhetorical questions to the Corinthians: "Am I not an apostle? Have I not seen Jesus our Lord? Are you not the result of my work in the Lord? Even though I may not be an apostle to others, surely I am to you!" (I Corinthians 9:1-2). In his epistle to the Galatians, he offers his apostolic credentials as they pertain to the three-year discipleship issue:

> I want you to know, brothers, that the gospel I preached is not
> something that man made up. I did not receive it from any man nor
> was I taught it; rather, I received it by revelation from Jesus Christ.
> . . . When God . . . was pleased to reveal his Son in me so that I
> might preach him among the Gentiles, I did not consult any man,
> nor did I go up to Jerusalem to see those who were apostles before I
> was, but I went immediately into Arabia and later returned to
> Damascus. Then after three years, I went up to Jerusalem to get
> acquainted with Peter and stayed with him fifteen days. (Galatians
> 1:11-18)

Paul claims here that he was indeed a personal disciple of Jesus, although he does not make clear how that instruction proceeded. Whether his specific mention of a three-year-time-period is significant or not is debatable.

To the Corinthians, he even claims to have learned specific details of Jesus' earthly life events directly from Jesus:

> For I received from the Lord that which I also passed on to you: The Lord Jesus, on the night in which he was betrayed, took bread, and when he had given thanks, he broke it and said, "This is my body which is for you; do this in remembrance of me." In the same way, after supper he took the cup, saying, "This cup is the new covenant in my blood; this do, as often as you drink it, in remembrance of me." (I Corinthians 11:23-25)

Paul asserts that he received this historical narrative from the Lord, not from others. Paul also points out that his apostleship is recognized by the other apostles: "James, Peter, and John, those reputed to be pillars, gave me and Barnabas the right hand of fellowship . . . They agreed that we should go to the Gentiles, and they to the Jews" (Galatians 2:9). If Paul's apostleship is recognized only after some difficulty, we should certainly not lightly accept the apostleship credentials of anyone living today. It is relatively safe to say that there are no modern-day apostles. That being said, it is safe to say that, since spiritual gifts were conferred by the laying on of apostles' hands, there are no modern-day spiritual gifts.

As I point out on pages 123-124 of *Psychotic Entelechy: The Dangers of Spiritual Gifts Theology*,

> The process of disseminating gifts would end when the last living apostle lays his hands on the last gift recipient before dying. . . . The process is complete (*teleios*). It will not be repeated in the future. The recipient has no power to pass on the gift

to anyone else. The New Testament contains no hint that anyone (other than an apostle) who possessed a spiritual gift could pass it on to someone else. . . . Following deductive reasoning, I assert the following:

- Major Premise: Spiritual gifts are only conferred by the laying on of apostles' hands.
- Minor Premise: There are no apostles living in the twenty-first century.
- Conclusion: There are no spiritual gifts in the twenty-first century.

On pages 95-98 of *Psychotic Entelechy: The Dangers of Spiritual Gifts Theology*, I offer a brief history of God's communication with humans:

I defined spiritual gifts as the receipt of messages from God. . . this is "history" as communicated from presumed spiritually gifted sources. The presumption is that much of the historic detail included would have relied on messages from God to certify its accuracy. Certainly, the Jewish Bible (the Christian Old Testament) accepts the premise that God spoke to and through certain individuals. That God spoke directly to Moses is the fundamental premise upon which Jewish Law is founded. The first five books of the Bible (Genesis, Exodus, Leviticus, Numbers, and Deuteronomy) are known as the Torah, the Hebrew word for Law. According to tradition, Moses is the essential author of all five books.

Genesis provides a rapid-fire account of more than two thousand years of human history prior to Israel's four-hundred-year sojourn in Egypt. Prior to the account of human history, Genesis offers a one-chapter account of the creation of heaven, earth, and the plant and animal kingdoms. Presumably, if Moses authored the creation and human history accounts, he would need some inspiration from God to certify that his account was accurate. Moses' account has God speaking directly to Adam and Eve, warning them not to eat of the Tree of the Knowledge of Good and

Evil. Following their Fall, God interrogates them and communicates to them their respective punishments. To their children, God signifies his preference for the animal sacrifices (of Abel) to the vegetable sacrifices (of Cain). Then, God warns Cain not to kill his brother. After Cain murders Abel, God personally interrogates Cain and tells Cain of his punishment. Later, God speaks to Noah, instructing him to build an Ark. After the Flood, God provides Noah and his family a brief list of laws. Then, God does not appear to communicate with humans until he begins to communicate with Abram, whom God renames Abraham.

In the final three-fourths of Genesis, God communicates frequently with Abraham and his family. God makes covenants with Abraham, his son Isaac, and Isaac's son Jacob, whom God renames Israel . . . Israel has twelve sons who become the patriarchs of the twelve tribes. One of those sons, Joseph, God takes special interest in, communicating with him through dreams. God has a special purpose in mind for Joseph, which takes Joseph to Egypt. His brothers sell him into slavery, but God causes him to rise to leadership in that land. Eventually, God uses Joseph's position of influence to rescue his father and his brothers' families from famine in the land of Canaan as they emigrate to Egypt. The entire account of Genesis, if authored by Moses, would require that Moses be inspired by God to be certified historically accurate. Moses' perspective was four hundred years removed from the most recent historical circumstances he reports on. The suggestion that Joseph may have written some accounts that Moses found in the Egyptian archives would argue for some historiographical accuracy, but none of the first five books make such an assertion.

Exodus begins with the Israelites still in Egypt four hundred years later. Now, the name of Joseph is long-forgotten by the Egyptians and the Israelites have become an enslaved people. God raises up an Israelite named Moses, educates him in Pharaoh's palace, and eventually speaks to him through a burning bush, commanding him to lead the Israelites out of Egypt and back to the Promised Land (of Canaan). God infuses Moses with miraculous powers and, upon his successful campaign to lead the children of Israel out of Egypt, God gives Moses the Law on Mount Sinai. The various laws and instructions God gives to Moses are detailed in Exodus, Leviticus, Numbers, and Deuteronomy. These four books pertain to historical issues occurring during the lifetime of Moses. The exception to this observation is the final chapter of Deuteronomy, which discusses the death of Moses. The primary purpose of spiritual gifts theology in the final four books (of Moses) is to certify the accuracy of Moses' messages concerning the Law. The Law (Torah) comes from God.

After Moses, there is a lesser profusion of spiritual giftedness throughout Jewish history. God speaks to Moses' successor Joshua throughout his leadership career in retaking the Land of Canaan. He performed miracles through Joshua—such as causing the Walls of Jericho to fall. After Joshua's death, God inspires and speaks to various judges—Othniel, Deborah, Gideon, Samson, and others. These judges receive miraculous abilities and counsel from God as they defend and protect Israelites in battle.

Although Moses, following God's Law, institutes the priesthood, it is not until later that the High Priest becomes the primary vehicle for God to communicate with humans. After the time of the Judges, God speaks to Samuel, as a child, and calls him into the priesthood. God continues to communicate messages to Samuel throughout his career. Samuel, with God's direction, anoints the first Israelite king, Saul. Then, Samuel, with God's direction anoints King David to replace Saul. The anointing of Samuel as priest (and the sense in which Samuel's anointing also made him a prophet) combined with the anointing of David as King (and the sense in which David's anointing also made him a prophet) introduces a new era in God's communication with humans. The three anointed (messianic) offices—prophet, priest, and king—become God's primary mouthpieces for Israel. The Hebrew word meaning "anointed one" is "messiah." (The Greek word meaning "anointed one," incidentally, is "christ.")

King David, under inspiration from God, writes many psalms. His son King Solomon, with similar inspiration, writes many proverbs. Later kings and priests are not considered to have equal inspiration. Later prophets, however, become the voice of God to Israel. The prophet Nathan was a contemporary of David. Elijah, Elisha, Micaiah, Isaiah, Jeremiah, Ezekiel, and Daniel are the most famous prophets. Other prophets whose writings are included in the Bible are: Hosea, Joel, Amos, Obadiah, Jonah, Micah, Nahum, Habakkuk, Zephaniah, Haggai, Zechariah, and Malachi. Pharisaic and Rabbinic Judaism and Christianity accept the premise that God spoke through these prophets . . . Pharisaic and Rabbinic Judaism believes that God's activity of speaking through prophets, however, ended with the canonical prophets of the Jewish Bible. Ezra the scribe instituted a new way for God to speak to Israel—through reading the Torah aloud to the people. Even though the age of the prophets ended with the canonical Tanach (or Old Testament) for the Jews, Pharisaic and Rabbinic Judaism still allowed for the possibility that God might speak through infants and fools.

Pharisaic and Rabbinic Judaism also taught that God could speak through a Bat Qol (or "mysterious voice"). This type of communication is claimed by the early Christians on a few occasions. When Jesus was baptized, a voice from Heaven said: "This is my son, whom I love; with him I am well pleased" (Matthew 3:17 NIV). When Jesus was transfigured, his disciples were startled by a bright cloud. A voice from the cloud said: "This is my son, whom I love; with him I am well pleased. Listen to him" (Matthew 17:5 NIV). When Saul of Tarsus (who later became the Apostle Paul) was confronted on the road to Damascus, he was blinded by a light from heaven and heard a voice saying: "Saul, Saul, why do you persecute me?" Saul asks who is speaking and the voice responds: "I am Jesus, whom you are persecuting . . . Now get up and go into the city, and you will be told what you must do" (Acts 9:5-6 NIV).

Christianity also believes that God continued to speak through the visitation of angels (as when Gabriel announced John's and Jesus' births) and through prophets and prophetesses such as Simeon and Anna (Luke 2:25-38) and especially through John the Baptist who lived at the time of Jesus. Christianity also teaches that God spoke through those (such as apostles and prophets) who had received spiritual gifts in the first generation of the church.

The Holy Spirit bats "cleanup." The Bible is NOT a thoroughly human book—written by humans without divine aid and collected and canonized by humans without divine aid. The logic of Christianity would be tenuous, indeed, if it were but a thoroughly human book. We may "load the bases" by arguing the logic that the New Testament books were historically and prophetically accurate, even by human historiographical standards. But, then the Holy Spirit steps up to bat. He hits a home run and clears (cleans up) the bases by certifying that the Bible is to be believed because, while it was written by humans using their own symbol systems, it was "inspired" by God. God must be true though every man be a liar (Romans 3:4--KJV). Christianity is thoroughly logical!

References

Aristotle (1991). *Aristotle on rhetoric: A theory of civic discourse*. G. A. Kennedy (Trans.). New York & Oxford: Oxford University Press.

Booth, W. (1974). *Modern dogma and the rhetoric of assent*. Chicago: University of Chicago Press.

Best, S. & Kellner, D. (1991). *Postmodern theory: Critical interrogations*. New York: Guilford Press.

Brandon, S. (1957). *The Fall of Jerusalem and the Christian Church*. London: S.P.C.K.

Burke, K. (1943). The five master terms: Their place in a "dramatistic" grammar of motives. [MT] *View* 3 (2), 50-52.

---. (1970). *The Rhetoric of religion: Studies in logology*. [RR] Berkeley: University of California Press.

---. (1966). *Language as symbolic action: Essays on life, literature, and method.* [LSA] Berkeley: University of California Press.

---. (1967). Dramatism. In L. Thayer (Ed.). *Communication: Concepts and perspectives* 327-360. [D] Washington, DC: Spartan.

---. (1968). *Counter-statement.* [CS] Berkeley: University of California Press.

---. (1969). *A grammar of motives.* [GM] Berkeley: University of California Press.

---. (1970). Poetics and communication. In H. E Kiefer and M. K. Munitz (Eds.), *Perspectives in education, religion, and the arts* 401-418. [P&C] Albany: State University of New York Press.

---. (1970). *The Rhetoric of religion: Studies in logology*. [RR] Berkeley: University of California Press.

---. (1972). *Dramatism and development.* [DD] Barre, MA: Clark University Press with Barre Publishers.

---. (1973a). *The philosophy of literary form: Studies in symbolic action* (3rd ed.). [PLF] Berkeley: University of California Press.

---. (1973b). The rhetorical situation. In L. Thayer (Ed.). *Communication: Ethical and moral issues* 263-275. [RS] London, New York, Paris: Gordon and Breach Science.

---. (1975). *Permanence and change: An anatomy of purpose* (2nd ed.). [PC] Indianapolis: Bobbs-Merrill Company, Inc.

---. (1984). *Attitudes toward history* (3rd ed.). [ATH] Berkeley: University of California Press.

Burrows, M. (1958). *More light on the Dead Sea Scrolls: New scrolls and new interpretations*. Viking Adult.

Caird, G. (1966). *The revelation of St John the Divine* (2nd ed). London: A & C Black.

Charles, R. (1923). *The British Academy lectures on the Apocalypse*. London: Oxford University Press.

---. (1975). *The revelation of St. John*. 2 vols. Of *The international critical commentary*. Edinburgh: T & T Clark.

Choi, C. Why Neanderthals likely fathered few kids with modern humans. *Live Science*. Retrieved from: http://www.livescience.com/54359-neanderthal-y-chromosome-caused-miscarriages.html.

Cicero? (1954). *Rhetorica ad Herennium*. Caplan, H. (Trans.). *Loeb Classical Library*, No. 403. Cambridge: Harvard University Press.

Clarke, R. & Delia, J. (1979). Topoi and rhetorical competence. *Quarterly journal of speech* 65 (2), 187-206.

Clifton, C. (1992). *Encyclopedia of Heresies and Heretics*. New York: Barnes & Noble Books.

Collins, A. (1984). *Crisis and catharsis: The power of the Apocalypse.* Philadelphia: Westminster.

Didymus, J.   Failed end-of-world predictions of Jesus' coming: Montanists and the Ecumenical Council (1000 A.D.) Retrieved from http://EzineArticles.com/5476263.

Fischel, H. (1973). *Rabbinic literature and Greco-Roman philosophy.* Leiden: E. J. Brill.

Fishman, I. (1970). *Gateway to the Mishnah.* Hartmore, CT: Prayer Book Press, Inc.

Foss, S. K., Foss, K. A., & Trapp, R. (2014). *Contemporary perspectives on rhetoric* (30th anniv. ed.). Long Grove, IL: Waveland.

Georgetown University Kennedy Institute of Ethics. (2015). Chapter 5: The Nazi eugenics programs.   In *High School bioethics curriculum project.* Retrieved from https://highschoolbioethics.georgetown.edu/units/cases/unit4_5.html.

Ghoniem, M. & M Saifullah. The Sacrifice Of Abraham: Isaac or Ishmael? In *Islamic awareness.* Retrieved   from: http://www.islamic-awareness.org/Quran/Contrad/MusTrad/sacrifice.html.

Homer. (1961). *The Iliad of Homer.* R. Lattimore, R. (Trans.). Chicago: University of Chicago Press.

Johnson, P. (2011). *Darwin on Trial* (20th anniv. ed.). Intervarsity Press, USA.

Kareem,   A.   The   Resurrection   Hoax.   Retrieved   from: http://answering-christianity.com/abdullah_smith/the_resurrection_hoax.htm)

Kirby, J. (1990). "The great triangle" in early Greek rhetoric and poetics. *Rhetorica: A journal of the history of rhetoric* 8 (3), 213-228.

Kittel, G. (Ed.). (1964). *Theological dictionary of the New Testament* (9 vols.). G. Bromiley (Trans.). Grand Rapids: Wm. G. Eerdmans.

Klausner, S. Z. (Ed.). (1968). *Why man takes chances: Studies in stress-seeking.* Garden City, NY: Doubleday.

Kuhn, T. (1962). *The structure of scientific revolutions.* Chicago: University of Chicago Press.

Lindeman, M., Heywood, B., Riekki, T., & Makkonen, T. (2014). Atheists become emotionally aroused when daring God to do terrible things. *International journal for the psychology of religion* 3 (2), 124-132.

Lindsay, S. (1977). *Anamartetous fallen angels.* Master's thesis. Bloomington: Indiana University.

---. (1997). Prayer as proto-rhetoric. *The journal of communication and religion* 20 (2), 31-40.

---. (1998). *Implicit rhetoric: Kenneth Burke's extension of Aristotle's concept of entelechy.* Lanham, MD: University Press of America.

---. (1999). Waco and Andover: An application of Kenneth Burke's concept of psychotic entelechy" *Quarterly journal of speech* 85 (3), 268-284.

---. (2001). *Revelation: The human drama.* Bethlehem, PA: Lehigh University Press.

---. (2004). *The seven Cs of stress: A Burkean approach.* Orlando: Say Press.

---. (2005). *Psychotic entelechy: The dangers of "spiritual gift" theology.* Lanham, MD: University Press of America.

---. (2009). *Persuasion, proposals, and public speaking* (2nd ed.). Orlando: Say Press.

---. (2010a). *Disneology: Religious rhetoric at Walt Disney World.* Orlando, FL: Say Press.

---. (2010b). *The rhetoric of Disney music.* Orlando, FL: Say Press.

---. (2014). *The expanded Kenneth Burke concordance.* Orlando: Say Press.

---. (2015a). *ArguMentor.* Orlando: Say Press.

---. (2015b). Burke, Perelman, and the transmission of values: The beatitudes as epideictic topoi. *KB journal* 11 (1).

---. (2015c). *Making offers they can't refuse: The twenty-one sales in a sale* (3rd ed.). Orlando: Say Press.

---. (2019a). *Angels and demons: The personification of communication.* Orlando: Say Press.

---. (2019b). *Hidden Mickeyisms: The implicit rhetoric of Disney films.* Orlando: Say Press.

McKeon, R. (1973). *Introduction to Aristotle* (2nd ed.). Chicago and London: University of Chicago Press.

Moriarty, S., N. Mitchell, & W. Wells. *Advertising and IMC: Principles and practice* (10th ed.). Upper Saddle River, NJ: Prentice Hall.

Muehlhauser, L. (2010). The Explosion of Early Christianity, Explained. In *Common sense atheism.* Retrieved from: http://commonsenseatheism.com/?p=95

Neher, W. W., Waite, D. H., Cripe, N., and Flood, R. E. (1994). *Public speaking: A rhetorical approach* (3rd ed.). Dubuque, IA: Kendall/Hunt.

Noll, M. (1986). *Between faith and criticism.* San Francisco: Harper & Row, Publishers.
.

Perelman, C. and L. Olbrechts-Tyteca. (1969). *The new rhetoric: A treatise on argumentation.* (J. Wilkinson and P. Weaver, Trans.). Notre Dame: University of Notre Dame Press.

Perelman, C. (1990). *The realm of rhetoric.* Notre Dame: University of Notre Dame Press.

Philo Judaeus. (1890). *The works of Philo Judaeus.* C. Yonge (Trans.). London: George Bell & Sons.

Plato (1968). *The republic.* B. Jowett (Trans.). New York: Airmont.

---. (1971). *Gorgias.* W. Hamilton (Trans.). London: Penguin.

---. (1973). *Phaedrus and the seventh and eighth letters*, W. Hamilton (Trans.). London: Penguin.

Plutarch (1950). Life of Alexander. In *Life Stories of men who shaped history from Plutarch's lives* 163-222. E. C. Lindeman (Ed.). W. Langhorne (Trans.). New York: New American Library.

The rise of the nation state during the Renaissance. In *The flow of history*. Retrieved from:
    http://www.flowofhistory.com/units/west/11/FC79.

Russell, J. (2018). *The parousia: A critical inquiry into the New Testament doctrine of our Lord's
    second coming*. Forgotten Books.

Smithsonian   Institute.   Human   origins.   Retrieved   from:
    http://humanorigins.si.edu/evidence/human-fossils/species/homo-sapiens.

Still, J. The problem with Jesus' arrest and trial. In *The Secular Web*. Retrieved from:
    http://infidels.org/library/modern/james_still/jesus_trial.html.

Strobel, L. (2016). *The case for Christ: A journalist's personal investigation of the evidence for
    Jesus*. Grand Rapids: Zondervan.

Talbert, C. (1977). *What is a gospel? The genre of the canonical gospels*. Philadelphia: Fortress
    Press.

---. (2010) *Matthew*. Ada, MI: Baker Academic.

Toulmin, S. E. (1964). *The uses of argument*. London: Cambridge University Press.

Weaver, R. M. (1953). *The ethics of rhetoric*. South Bend, IN: Henry Regnery.

Index

Parousia v, 66-67, 135-145, 148, 151, 153, 155, 157, 165, 185

Passover 59, 62, 189

Pathos viii

Pentad 38, 40

People of the Book 58

Perelman, Chaim 27, 105-106, 175-176, 190

Pharisees 83, 85, 89, 115-116, 208

Phenomenon/a 33, 45, 125, 182, 199

Philippians Hymn 65, 74-75

Philo 37

Physics 123-124, 130

Planned Parenthood 54

Pleasure 60, 63, 150

Political 84, 113, 172

Pontius Pilate 78, 103, 157

Pope Francis 3-4, 99, 108

Postmodern/ism 14, 21-23, 26, 29, 42, 105, 108, 149

Prayer 156, 199-200

Premise/s vii, 10-12, 25-26, 32, 37, 73, 107-109, 123, 135, 186, 190, 205, 208

Presumption ix, 105-110, 114, 119, 123, 144, 148, 151, 155, 176, 190-191, 205

www.ingramcontent.com/pod-product-compliance
Lightning Source LLC
Chambersburg PA
CBHW080459110426
42742CB00017B/2935